Publishing Details

This first edition published July 2002 by
The Tipbook Company bv, The Netherlands.

Distributed exclusively by the Hal Leonard Corporation,
7777 West Bluemound Road, P.O. Box 13819
Milwaukee, Wisconsin 53213.

Typeset in Glasgow and Minion.

Printed in The Netherlands by Hentenaar Boek bv, Nieuwegein.

144pp

ISBN 90-76192-47-2

Hugo Pinksterboer

Tipbook
Cello

Handy, clearly written, and up-to-date.
The reference manual for both beginning and advanced
cellists, including Tipcodes and a glossary.

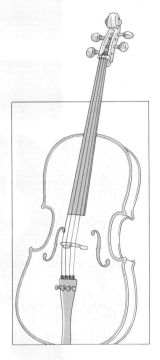

THE **TIPBOOK**
COMPANY

THE BEST GUIDE TO YOUR INSTRUMENT!

Thanks

For their information, their expertise, their time, and their help we'd like to thank the following musicians, teachers, technicians, and other bowed instrument experts: Edward C. Campbell (violin maker, PA), Duane Lightner (Discount String Center, IN), Lang Shen (Knilling String Instruments, MO), David Rivinus (violin maker, OR), Caryn Patterson (Super-Sensitive Strings, FL), Heinz Kovacs (Thomastik-Infeld, Austria), Sandy Neill (D'Addario, NY), Volker Müller-Zierach (Pirastro, Germany), Klaus Clement (Höfner, Germany), Barbara Van Itallie (Violin Society of America), Kim Rodney and Frederik Habel (Gewa, Germany), Barbara Woldring, Michaël van Berkum (violin maker), Ben de Ligt, Levent Aslan, Isabelle van Keulen, Nello Mirando, Theo Olof, Mies Albarda (European String Teachers Association (ESTA/ARCO), Jaap Bolink (violin maker), Gijs van Ulsen, Taner Erkek, Harm van der Geest, Siard de Jong, Fred Lindeman (violin maker), Annelies Steinhauer (violin maker), Eduard van Tongeren (violin maker), Helena and Jelle van Tongeren, Tom van Berkel, Bas van den Broek, and Fred Pinksterboer. We also wish to thank Frank Pameijer for his musical help in making the Tipcode-movies. The cello on the cover is played by Davina Cowan.

Anything missing?

Any omissions? Any areas that could be improved? Please go to www.tipbook.com to contact us; thanks!

Acknowledgements

Concept, design, and illustrations: Gijs Bierenbroodspot

Cover photo: René Vervloet

Editor: Robert L. Doerschuk

Proofreader: Nancy Bishop

IN BRIEF

Have you just started playing? Are you thinking about buying a cello? Or do you want to find out more about the instrument you already have? If so, this book will tell you everything you need to know. About buying or renting an instrument, about tailpieces, tuning pegs, bridges, and fingerboards, about bows, strings, and tuning. About the best way to maintain your instrument, about the history of the cello, about its family, and much, much more.

The best you can
Having read this Tipbook, you'll be able to get the most out of your instrument, to buy the best cello you can, and to easily grasp any other literature on the subject, from magazines to books and Internet publications.

The first four chapters
If you have just started playing, or haven't yet begun, pay particular attention to the first four chapters. Have you been playing longer? Then skip ahead to Chapter 5.
Please note that all prices mentioned in this book reflect only approximate street prices in US dollars.

Glossary
Most of the cello terms you'll come across in this book are briefly explained in the glossary at the end. To make life even easier, it doubles as an index.

Hugo Pinksterboer

CONTENTS

SEE WHAT YOU READ WITH TIPCODE

www.tipbook.com

In addition to the many illustrations on the following pages, Tipbooks offer you a new way to see – and even hear – what you are reading about. The Tipcodes that you will come across regularly in this book give you access to extra pictures, short movies, soundtracks, and other additional information at www.tipbook.com.

How it works is very simple. One example: On page 90 of this book you can read about fitting new strings. Right above that paragraph it says **Tipcode CELLO-017**.
Type in that code on the Tipcode page at www.tipbook.com and you will see a short movie that shows you how to do this.

Enter code, watch movie
You enter the Tipcode below the movie window on the Tipcode page. In most cases, you will then see the relevant images within five to ten seconds. Tipcodes activate a short movie, sound, or both, or a series of photos.

Tipcodes listed
For your convenience, all the Tipcodes used in this book are shown in a single list on page 124.

Quick start
The Tipcode movies, photo series, and soundtracks are designed so that they start quickly. If you miss something the first time, you can of course repeat them. And if it all happens too fast, you can use the pause button below the movie window.

First, make your selection: Tipcode, chords, and fingering charts, or the glossary.

The Tipcode window displays movies, photo series, fingering charts, chords, and explanations of the words used in this book.

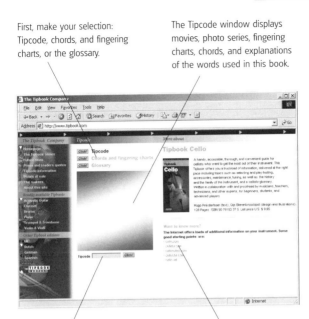

Enter a Tipcode here and click on the button. Want to see it again? Click again.

These links take you directly to other interesting sites.

Plug-ins

If the software you need to view the movies or photos is not yet installed on your computer, you'll automatically be told which software you need, and where you can download it. This kind of software (*plug-ins*) is free.

Still more at www.tipbook.com

You can find even more information at www.tipbook.com. For instance, you can look up words in the glossaries of all the Tipbooks published to date. For flutists, clarinetists, and saxophonists there are fingering charts, for drummers there are the rudiments, and for guitarists and pianists there are chord diagrams. Also included are links to some of the websites mentioned in the *Want to Know More?* section of each Tipbook.

1. A CELLIST?

As a cellist, you can play solo, all by yourself, or in a duet with a pianist or another cellist. You can also play in a symphony orchestra, with dozens of other musicians. There are countless other types of groups and ensembles you can join as well, playing classical music, or perhaps jazz, or yet another style of music. A chapter about all the things you can do as a cellist.

At first sight, cellos look a lot like violins. They're a lot bigger, though, and they sound lower. When you play the cello, it rests between your legs, standing on a rod.

String instrument

The cello is a *string instrument*, just like the violin. You play these instruments by drawing a bow across the strings. That's why they're also known as *bowed instruments*.

The voice

The sound of a cello is often said to resemble the human voice. The highest sounding string of the cello is even known as the *chanterelle* – in English, the singing string.

Wide range
Tipcode Cello-001

That is just one of the reasons why cellists can be found in so many different groups and ensembles. Another is that their instrument can sound both very low and extremely high: The cello has a very wide *range*. Also, its tone blends well with a wide variety of instruments, from woodwinds such as the flute or the clarinet, to the piano, the accordion, other string instruments, and – of course – the human voice.

1

Different styles

Most cellists play classical music, but you'll find them in many other styles too – in folk music from different countries, in gypsy music, the tango and French chansons, in jazz and pop, and in avant-garde music, for example.

This is how you play the cello.

Classical music

There is a wide variety of classical cello music available. That's not surprising, because the instrument has been around for centuries. All in all there is so much cello music that you couldn't play it in a lifetime.

Large and small

Classical music can be played in large and small orchestras, in quartets, and in many other kinds of groups and ensembles. Here are some examples.

Symphony orchestra

The strings are the main voices of the largest orchestra of all, the symphony orchestra, which has a total of fifty to a hundred or more members. In a symphony orchestra, the cellists are usually seated to the right of the conductor. On the conductor's immediate right is the *principal cellist*, who leads the cello section. On the conductor's left hand is the *concertmaster*, a violinist who is the leader of the entire orchestra.

String sections

The cellists are one of the five groups of string instrument players in the orchestra. The largest group is the violinists, of whom there may be thirty or more, divided into *first* and *second violinists*. The *violists*, a smaller string section, play the slightly bigger and lower-sounding *viola*. Behind the cellists are the *bassists*. Their instrument, the double bass, is the one of the lowest voices of the orchestra.

String orchestras

The four string sections of a symphony orchestra are not unlike the different groups of singers in a choir: sopranos, altos, tenors (the cellists), and basses. So it shouldn't be a surprise that there are string orchestras too, made up of string players only.

Cello orchestras

Also, there's music written or adapted for cello orchestras, with fifty or even more cellists, and for smaller cello ensembles, with songs and compositions that range from tangos to Spanish folk songs, Christmas carols, hymns, and even heavy-metal hits.

Other musicians

In a symphony orchestra you'll find other musicians as well, such as brasswind players (playing trumpet, French horn, trombone, and other instruments), woodwind players (clarinet, flute, oboe, bassoon, and so on), percussionists (snare drums, tympani, cymbals), harpists, a pianist… As you can see, the louder instruments, such as the trumpets and percussion instruments, are further toward the back; the strings are closer to the audience.

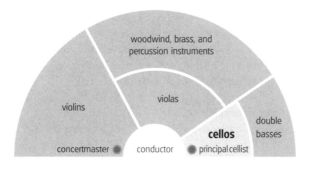

An example of the arrangement of the instruments in a symphony orchestra. The cellos are nearly always at the front, to the right of the conductor.

String quartet

A lot of classical music has been written for smaller groups too. A well-known and very popular ensemble is the string quartet, for instance, with two violinists, a violist, and a cellist. A string quintet has two cellists or two violists. Piano

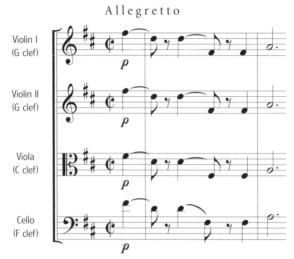

Allegretto

Violin I (G clef)

Violin II (G clef)

Viola (C clef)

Cello (F clef)

A few bars from a string quartet (W. A. Mozart); music for two violins, viola, and cello.

trios are written for piano, violin, and cello; for a piano quartet you add a viola.

Duo and solo

There is also a lot of music for duos. The most popular combination is cello and piano, but you can also play with another cellist, for example, or with a clarinetist or an accordion player. And there are pieces that are meant to be played solo – just a cello, and nothing else. Of course, that's a different type of solo playing than when you play 'solo' cello accompanied by a full orchestra.

Cello or violoncello?

Most musicians call a cello a cello, but some use the older name of the instrument, *violoncello*. In the past, the cello has had many other names as well. You'll find more about this and the instrument's history in Chapter 11, *Back in Time*.

Sello or chello?

The cello is an Italian instrument, originally. That's why most musicians pronounce its name as 'chello,' as Italians would say it. Others say 'sello,' and both are right. Similarly, if you're talking about more than one cello, you can say 'celli' – the Italian way – or 'cellos.'

2. A QUICK TOUR

A cello has a body, a neck, and a fingerboard, four strings, four pegs, and a whole list of other parts. A chapter about what everything's called, what it's for and where to find it, and about cellos for children.

The main part of the cello, the *body*, is the soundbox of the instrument: It amplifies the sound of the strings. Without the body, you would hardly hear yourself play.

Top and back
The *top* and the *back* of the body are noticeably arched. The top is the most important part for the sound of the instrument. It has two large *f*-shaped *soundholes*, also known as *f-holes*.

Tuning pegs
You tune the strings using the *pegs* or *tuning pegs*. There is one for each string, at the top of the instrument, fitted in the *pegbox*.

Scroll
Right at the top is the *scroll* or *volute*. Some cellos have the head of a lion, a woman, or an angel instead of a regular scroll.

Fingerboard   Tipcode CELLO-003
The strings run along the *fingerboard* onto which you press your fingers to *stop the strings*. If you stop a string you make it shorter, so to speak. This makes the string produce a higher note.

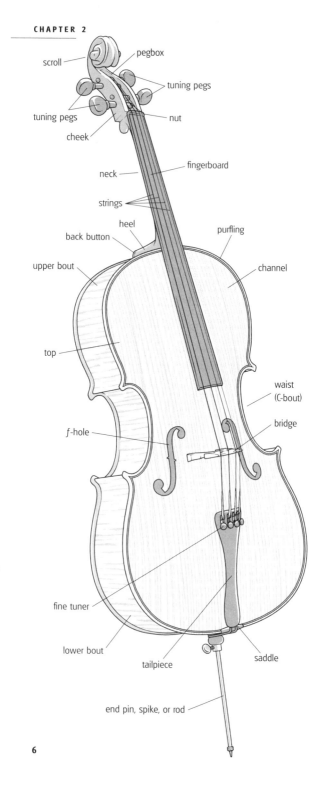

scroll

pegbox

tuning pegs

tuning pegs

nut

cheek

neck

fingerboard

strings

heel

purfling

back button

upper bout

channel

top

waist
(C-bout)

f-hole

bridge

fine tuner

lower bout

tailpiece

saddle

end pin, spike, or rod

The neck

The fingerboard is a thin, dark plank that's glued to the *neck*. The neck runs from the scroll to the body. The fingerboard is quite a bit longer: A large part juts out over the body.

Nut

At the top of the fingerboard, the strings run over a small ridge called the *nut*.

The bridge

About halfway down the body, the strings run over the *bridge*, a thin piece of wood that's much lighter in color than the rest of the cello. When you play, you make the strings vibrate with your bow. The bridge passes on those vibrations to the top. The top, together with the rest of the body, amplifies the sound.

Feet

The bridge stands on the top on its two *feet*, without the help of glue or screws. The pressure of the strings keeps it from falling over.

Tailpiece and fine tuners

The strings are attached to the pegs at one end and to the *tailpiece* at the other. Inside the tailpiece there are often one or more *fine tuners*, which allow you to tune your cello more easily and precisely than with the big wooden tuning pegs.

Button, loop, and saddle

The tailpiece is attached to the (*end*) *button* with the *tailpiece loop*. To make sure this loop doesn't damage the body, it runs over the *saddle* or *bottom nut*.

Fittings

The tailpiece, pegs, and end pin plug are collectively known as the *fittings* or the *trim*.

End pin

The rod of the end pin takes most of the weight of the cello, when you play. Adjusting its height is simply a matter of how far you pull it out. When you're done playing, you retract the rod into the instrument.

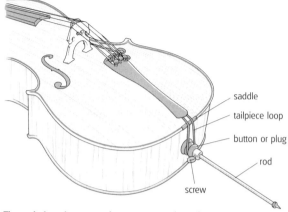

saddle

tailpiece loop

button or plug

rod

screw

The end pin: a button or plug, a screw, and a rod.

Purfling

The inlaid *purfling* runs along the edge of the body. It is usually made of three narrow strips of wood – two ebony or dark dyed strips, and a lighter wood in between.

Channel

From the edge, the top usually dips a little, before the upward arching begins. This 'valley' is called the *channel*. The back has almost the same shape.

Heel and shoulder

The semicircular part that sticks out at the top of the back is called the *heel*. The shoulder, the wider bottom part of the neck that links it to the body, is glued to the heel.

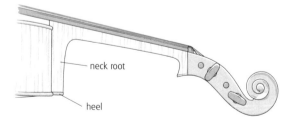

neck root

heel

INSIDE

There is plenty to see inside a cello too, from the sound post to the bass bar, the maker's label, and a number of small wooden blocks.

The sound post

If you look through the *f*-hole at the treble side of the instrument (by the thinnest string), you can see a length of round wood, wedged between the top and the back. That's the *sound post*. Without it, a cello would sound very thin or hollow.

The bass bar

Near the other *f*-hole, on the bass side, is the *bass bar*. This strengthens the top and it enhances the lower frequencies of the instrument. If you can take the rod of the end pin out of your instrument, you'll be able to see both the bass bar and the sound post through the hole in the end pin plug.

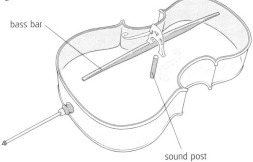

bass bar

sound post

The bass bar and sound post are important to the sound of a cello.

The label

If you look down the *f*-hole on the bass side, you may see the violin maker's label. Violin maker? Yes: The people who make cellos are known as *violin makers*. Usually, they make violins, violas, and cellos, and sometimes double basses too. Violin makers are also referred to as *luthiers*.

THE BOW

To play the cello you need a bow. The quality of the bow is as important as the quality of the instrument itself.

Bow hair and stick

The *bow hair* – usually more than two hundred hairs – almost always comes from a horse's tail. One end of the hair is held in place inside the *head* or *tip*, at the top end

head

stick

bow hair

winding

bow grip

frog

screw
button

of the *stick* or *bow stick*. The other end is held in place inside the *frog*.

Tension the hair

Before you play, you have to tension the hair by turning the *screw button* clockwise. After you have finished playing, turn the screw button counterclockwise until the hair goes slack. If you don't, the stick's elasticity will gradually decrease.

Bow grip

You hold the bow at the (*bow*) grip, often made of leather, and the *winding*, usually made of very thin metal wire. Apart from improving your bow hold, this also protects the wood.

Rosin

For the bow to do its job properly, you need to rub the hair with a piece of *rosin*. Rosin makes the bow hair slightly sticky. Without it, sliding the bow across the strings will hardly produce a sound.

STRINGS AND CLEFS

A cello has four strings. Most cellists use strings with a steel core; others prefer strings with a synthetic or a gut core. If you take a closer look, you can see that the strings are usually wound with ultra-thin metal ribbon.

The notes

The cello strings are tuned to the notes C, G, D, and A, as shown on the piano keyboard on the next page. The C is the lowest sounding string; the thin A-string is the highest.

Very low, very high

If you go from the lowest to the very

highest note you can play on a cello, you will span more than five octaves. (An octave is eight white keys on a piano.) This means that a cello has a wider range than most other instruments.

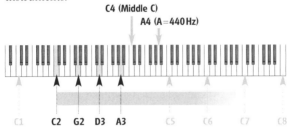

The four cello strings and the range of the instrument, pictured on a piano keyboard.

A3

As you can see in the illustration, the A-string of a cello sounds the same pitch as the A to the left of the Middle C. This particular A is indicated as A3. It sounds one octave lower than A4, the pitch to which most musicians tune their instruments.

Lower case

In classical literature, you may find A3 being indicated with the lower-case letter a, and A4 as a'.

Clefs

If you take another look at the music on page 4, you'll see that each stave is marked with a different symbol for each different instrument. This symbol is called a *clef*. The music for the violins is written using the *treble clef* or *G clef*. The music for the cello has a *bass clef* or *F clef*, and the alto violin uses the *alto clef*. With each clef, the lines of the staff indicate different notes.

All three

Because of the wide range of the instrument, you can't write cello music using the bass clef alone. The highest notes on the cello are written using the treble clef – just like the violin – and for in-between notes there's the *tenor clef* (a C clef with Middle C on the second line from the top). As a cellist, you will eventually have to learn to read music in these three clefs.

CHILDREN'S INSTRUMENTS

A full-size cello is too big for most children under twelve to fourteen years of age. That's why there are cellos in small or *fractional sizes.*

Full-size cello

An 'adult' cello is usually referred to as a *full-size cello.* On paper this is often indicated as a ¼ cello. The illustration below shows that a ½ cello is not really half as big as a ¼ instrument. Besides the ones shown here, there are other fractional sizes as well.

No rules

There are no absolute rules for which size goes with which age. One six-year-old might be better off with a ¼ cello while another child of that age needs a ½ instrument. That's why you always need to 'fit' a cello, and the same goes for

| **1/8** | **1/4** | **1/2** |
| (19.29"/490mm) | (21.06"/535mm) | (23.62"/600mm) |

The most popular cello sizes and their average string lengths (measured from nut to bridge).

the bow. A teacher will know how, and so will a good violin dealer or maker. Not only the child's finger and arm lengths count, but also factors such as the strength of their fingers.

Variations
The sizes of the instruments also vary: For example, one ½ cello may be slightly bigger or smaller than the other.

Smaller
As smaller cellos have a 'smaller' tone, you shouldn't play an instrument that is 'too small' for you. Having said that, if you're absolutely in love with the sound of your ⅞ cello, you may prefer that instrument to a full-size – until you find one you like even better…

3/4	7/8	4/4
(25.00"/635 mm)	(26.34"/670 mm)	(27.36"/695 mm)

3. LEARNING TO PLAY

The cello may not be the easiest instrument to get started on, but it won't take years before you can perform on it. A chapter about learning to play, lessons, and practicing.

Anyone can play any note on a piano: Just hit the right key, and it sounds. On a cello it's a bit harder. Producing a nice and even tone by drawing the bow over the strings will definitely take you some time.

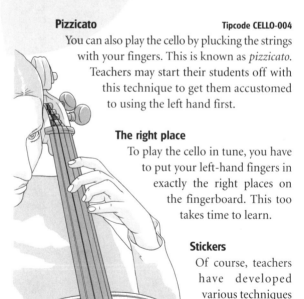

Pizzicato

Tipcode CELLO-004

You can also play the cello by plucking the strings with your fingers. This is known as *pizzicato*. Teachers may start their students off with this technique to get them accustomed to using the left hand first.

The right place

To play the cello in tune, you have to put your left-hand fingers in exactly the right places on the fingerboard. This too takes time to learn.

Stickers

Of course, teachers have developed various techniques to make learning the cello less hard than it may sound

Finding the exact place...

here – and there are thousands of young cellists to demonstrate that it can be done. One of the techniques used is simply to mark the positions where to put your left-hand on the fingerboard with stickers.

LESSONS

If you take cello lessons, you'll learn about everything connected with playing the instrument – from bowing technique and reading music to a good posture.

Locating a teacher

Are your looking for a private teacher? Violin makers and dealers may be able to refer you to a cello teacher, and music stores may have teachers on staff. You can also consult your local Musicians' Union, or the band director at the high school in your vicinity. You may also check the classified ads in newspapers, in music magazines, or on supermarket bulletin boards, or consult the *Yellow Pages*. Professional private teachers will usually charge between twenty-five and seventy-five dollars per hour. Some make house calls, for which you'll pay extra.

Group or individual lessons

Instead of taking individual lessons, you can also go for group lessons if that's an option in your vicinity. Private lessons are more expensive, but can be tailored exactly to your needs.

Collectives

You also may want to check whether there are any teachers' collectives or music schools in your vicinity. These collectives may offer extras such as ensemble playing, master classes, and clinics, in a wide variety of styles and at various levels.

Questions, questions

On your first visit to a teacher, don't simply ask how much it costs. Here are some other useful questions.
- Is an **introductory lesson** included? This is a good way to find out how well you get on with the teacher and, for that matter, with the instrument.
- Is the teacher interested in taking you on as a student if

you are just doing it for the fun of it, or are you expected to practice **at least three hours** a day?

- Do you have to make a large investment in method books right away, or is **course material provided**?
- Can you **record your lessons**, so that you can listen at home to how you sound, and once more to what has been said?
- Is this teacher going to make you practice scales for two years, or will you be **pushed onto a stage** as soon as possible?

PRACTICE

How long should you practice? That depends on your talent and on what you want to achieve. As an indication: Half an hour a day usually results in steady progress. If playing half an hour at a stretch seems too long, try dividing it up into two quarter-hour sessions, or three of ten minutes each.

A practice mute   Tipcode CELLO-005

Cellos don't make a lot of noise, but they are loud enough to bother other people when you are practicing. There are various ways to overcome this. First of all, you can buy a *practice mute*, available in wood, metal, or rubber, for some ten to fifteen dollars. You simply slide this short, fat 'comb' onto the bridge of your cello, where it effectively mutes most of the sound you produce – so it's best not to use one if you're working on your tone. Other types of mutes are covered in Chapter 8.

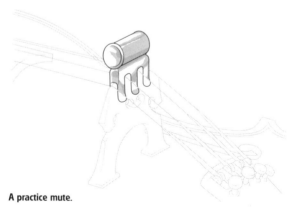

A practice mute.

Electric cello

If you want to produce even less sound, you may want to invest in an electric cello. Some of these instruments have been specifically designed for silent practicing. You play them using a pair of headphones; the extremely modest sound of the strings is amplified by a small built-in amp. A special input allows you to hook up a CD player, for instance, so you can play along with prerecorded music. There's more on electric cellos in Chapter 12, *The Family*.

On CD

Most cello music is played together with other string instruments, with a piano, or with a complete orchestra. There's an easy way to get hold of those other musicians, without having to invite them all: For instance, you can get special practice CDs with the same piece of music recorded three times. The first time very slowly with piano and cello, so that you can play along with the cellist. The next time faster with just the piano. Then once more with a full orchestra, in the tempo in which the piece is supposed to be played. These CDs usually come with sheet music.

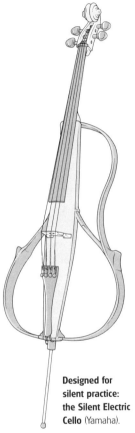

Designed for silent practice: the Silent Electric Cello (Yamaha).

Your computer

There are also CD-ROMs you can play along to. Of course, you will need to have a computer handy. Some CD-ROMs even let you decide how fast a piece should be played or whether you want to mute the cello part.

Metronome

Most pieces of music are supposed to be played in the same tempo from beginning to end. Playing with a metronome now and then helps you to learn how to play at a constant tempo. A metronome is a small mechanical or electronic device that ticks or bleeps out a steady adjustable pulse, so you can tell immediately if you're dragging or speeding.

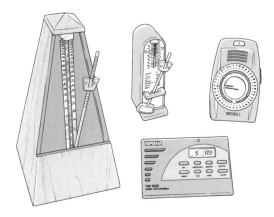

Two mechanical and two electronic metronomes.

Recording your lessons

If you record your lessons, you can listen to what was said, and especially to how you sounded, when you get home. You can learn a lot by listening to yourself playing. That's why many musicians record themselves. All you need is a cassette recorder with a built-in microphone – but better equipment yields better and more enjoyable results.

Listen and play

Finally, visit festivals, concerts, and other performances. Go watch and listen to orchestras, string quartets, and other groups. One of the best ways to learn to play is seeing other musicians at work. Living legends or local amateurs – every concert's a learning experience. And the best way to learn to play? Play a lot!

4. BUYING OR RENTING?

What does a cello cost? Somewhere between a few hundred and a few million dollars... A guide to cello prices, and to buying or renting an instrument.

Children under twelve often start off on a rented cello, which is easy to exchange for a larger size after you've grown a bit. Even if you are well beyond that age, renting a cello can be a good way to start, to find out either if you like playing the instrument at all, or if you like a specific instrument.

Rental fees

You can rent a full-sized student cello from around forty dollars a month, complete with bow and case, and some companies even rent out instruments for some hundred and fifty dollars for an academic year. Insurance may be included. If not, insurance rates for student instruments are usually under ten dollars per month. Fractional-sized instruments are not always cheaper to rent. Some stores may ask for a deposit; others require your credit card number.

Rent-to-own

Some companies offer a rent-to-own program: If you choose to buy an instrument later on, the rental fee, or part of it, will be applied against the price. There's a wide and pretty confusing variety of rental and rent-to-own programs, so always read the agreement carefully before you sign it, and compare what various dealers or music stores are offering.

Try before you buy

It's also possible to rent a more expensive instrument, so you can take your time to assess its quality. To give you an idea, you may rent a forty-thousand-dollar cello for six hundred dollars per month (*i.e.*, 1.5% of the list price).

BUYING A CELLO?

If you're looking for a decent, good-sounding cello that you can enjoy playing for a number of years, many dealers and teachers will tell you to spend some fourteen hundred to two thousand dollars or more, and add at least another three to four hundred for a basic bow and a case.

Cheaper instruments

Of course, plenty of people have had years of fun playing a much cheaper instrument. After all, you can buy a complete *outfit* (cello, bow, and case) for as little as four hundred dollars, or even less. That said, there are cheap cellos that are barely playable unless you have a lot of work done to them – even if they are labeled 'manufacturer adjusted.'

Shop adjustment

Basically, every production cello needs an additional shop adjustment before it can be played. This adjustment, commonly known as *setting up the instrument*, includes making sure that the bridge, nut, sound post, fingerboard, and tuning pegs perfectly fit the instrument.

Better, finer, richer

If you buy a more expensive cello, the higher price probably means that more time and attention has been devoted to its manufacture, that better wood has been used and that all the components are better matched to each other. Altogether that goes to make a better-looking, richer-sounding instrument, which may well be easier – and more fun and more rewarding – to play.

Better but cheaper

That said, you may very well find a new thousand-dollar instrument that performs and looks better than a new one priced at fifteen hundred dollars, depending, for one thing, on where the instrument was made.

A good sound for less

The most important tip when you go to buy your first instrument is to take someone along who knows something about it. He or she will be able to tell you if a cello sounds much better than its price suggests, or the other way around. If you don't know a cellist you can take along, try asking your teacher. And if you can't find anyone at all, at least buy a cello from someone who plays the instrument.

STUDENT AND MASTER CELLOS?

All kinds of names are used to classify cellos. What's what, and what do these names mean?

To begin with...

For example, you may find cellos classified as student, orchestra, and concert instruments. These names seem to suggest that you should start off with the first, buy an orchestra cello once you are good enough to play in an orchestra, and move on to a concert cello as soon as you're ready to play a solo concert... Similarly, there are conservatory and artist cellos.

Problem

The problem with these names is that everyone has their own ideas about what they mean. For instance, some master violin makers build 'student cellos' that sell for ten times the price of a mass-produced 'concert cello.' So don't pay too much attention to the names. The price will usually tell you more.

Handmade

'Handmade' is another word that can be misleading. Plenty of low-cost production cellos have largely or entirely been built by hand – but that doesn't necessarily mean they're good instruments.

Master cellos

The term 'master cello' can be just as vague. Officially, though, master cellos are made from start to finish by a master violin maker. They usually cost some ten thousand dollars or more, and you'd have to be prepared to join a year-long waiting list for delivery. It goes without saying that a

master violin maker or *luthier* does everything by hand –
so the word 'handmade' would be redundant in this case.

Workshop cellos

The term *workshop cello* usually refers to instruments
that others may call intermediate or step-up cellos, in the
price range of about twelve hundred dollars and more.
These are often good, handmade instruments, but they're
produced by a team of workers, rather than by one master
luthier.

Old production instruments

Older factory-made cellos can fetch a relatively high price,
because many cellists believe that old instruments sound
better, or that they're 'the real thing.' Even so, a brand new
cello costing twelve hundred dollars may well be a better
instrument than an eighteen-hundred-dollar cello that
was built in the early 1900s, for example.

Small cellos

Fractional-sized cellos are not always that much (if any)
cheaper than full-sized instruments of the same quality.
The same goes for bows, strings, and cases.

True story

A true story. A violinist goes to buy an expensive violin. He
plays, looks, and listens, plays and listens some more, and
then he makes his choice: This violin is the one for him.
But he doesn't buy it because, to his shock and surprise, he
is told that he picked the cheapest instrument available,
priced at only ten thousand dollars – and he was actually
looking for an instrument of at least five times that price.
Similar stories are told about cellists too …

BUYING TIPS

The main buying tip? Always buy your instrument from
people who understand – and love – cellos, as they won't
send you home with a barely playable instrument. Also,
they will be able to guide you in the sometimes confusing
world of the cello, with its numerous brand names and
countries of origin. Chapter 14 tells you more about cello
brands and makers.

Where to buy?

You can buy cellos in general music stores, which often sell mainly lower-priced production instruments, or from specialized violin dealers and violin makers. Besides expensive handmade (master) cellos, many violin makers supply more affordable instruments too.

On approval

In some cases you may be able to take an instrument on approval, so that you can assess it at your leisure. This is more common with expensive instruments than cheap ones, and you are more likely to be offered this opportunity if you are a good cellist than if you are choosing your first instrument.

Label

You can buy good cellos through the classified ads in the paper or at auctions, if you know what to look for. A word of warning, though: There are thousands of cellos around with labels bearing the name Stradivarius, or the names of other famous violin makers. Anyone can make labels. Making cellos is harder.

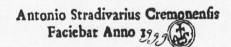

Just about anyone can make a label...

Appraisal

If you find a secondhand instrument anywhere else than at a reputable violin dealer or maker, it's best to have it appraised before you buy. Violin makers can usually tell you exactly what a cello should cost. They'll also tell you anything that's wrong with it, and what it will cost to put it right. An appraisal may cost one or more percent of the value of the cello. If that doesn't amount to much, you may have to pay a minimum charge instead.

Buying online

You can also buy musical instruments online or by mail-order. This makes it impossible to compare instruments.

Online and mail-order companies usually offer a return service for most or all of their products: If you're not happy with your purchase, you can send it back within a certain period of time. Of course the instrument should be in new condition when you send it back.

Time

Take your time when you go to buy a cello. After all, you want it to last you for a long time. Only if you fall totally in love with an instrument should you buy it straight away. Or perhaps a week or two later, or once you can afford it…

Fairs and conventions

One last tip: If a string players' or educators' convention is being held in your vicinity, try to attend it. Besides lots of instruments you can try out and compare, you will also come across plenty of product specialists, as well as numerous fellow cellists who are always a good source of information and inspiration.

MORE AND MORE EXPENSIVE

Professional cellists and conservatory students often play instruments worth tens of thousands of dollars, and there are even cellos that cost two million or more. How do they get so expensive?

Like paintings

Cellos by Stradivarius, Amati, Guarnerius, and other famous makers of the past don't cost so much only because they're so good, but also because they're some three hundred years old: They're rare, just like the famous great paintings from that era.

Better?

Though age doesn't necessarily make cellos better, it does make them more expensive. You can easily pay ten times as much – or more – for a high-quality old instrument as for an equally good new one. More than once, the sound of a new cello was preferred to that of a famous million-dollar-instrument in blindfold tests, but this will never really influence the price of the old masters.

Less famous, less expensive

The price of an old cello also depends on how well known the maker is. You may be able to buy a very good, rare German cello that's the same age as a Stradivarius for less than twenty thousand dollars.

Reasonable?

When discussing old and expensive cellos, you need to watch out with words like good, bad, or reasonable. For every expert who claims that you can get a 'reasonable cello' for some ten thousand dollars, you'll be able to find another expert who will say that 'reasonable' starts at no less than seventy-five grand.

A few years or fifteen minutes

Likewise, some experts claim that a new cello will start sounding really good after a few years of playing, while others say it takes fifteen minutes at most; and some experts believe in the use of special vibrating devices that 'break in' your instrument for you, while others don't.

5. A GOOD CELLO

When you first start playing, all cellos seem to look and sound the same. This chapter shows you the differences between them and tells you how to play-test them, covering varnishes and wood, sizes, tops, backs, bridges, pegs, and all other details of the instrument – as well as its sound, of course.

How a cello sounds depends a lot on how it was built and on the quality of the wood. But the strings are important too, and so is the bow, and the adjustment of the instrument. These three subjects are dealt with in Chapters 6 (*Good strings*), 7 (*Bows and rosins*), and 10 (*Cello maintenance*).

Purely by ear

The first and major part of this chapter is about everything there is to see on a cello, and what it all means for how the instrument sounds. If you prefer to choose a cello using your ears only, then you can skip ahead to the tips on pages 43–47.

THE LOOKS

Cellos come in glossy and matte finishes, and some instruments have a warm, satin-like glaze. When it comes to their color, there are even more variations. Some are pale orange or even yellowish, others have a rich amber or a deep brown hue, and still others tend toward red or purple. Cellos in completely different colors, such as green or blue, are very rare – but you can find them.

Oil and spirit

Traditionally, cellos have an oil-based finish, which used to take weeks to dry. Today, these finishes can be dried using ultraviolet light, and you may be able to find oil-varnished cellos for as little as eight hundred dollars. Spirit-based varnishes are used on cellos in most price ranges, often hand-rubbed rather than being sprayed or brushed. Be aware that spirit- and oil-based finishes on inexpensive instruments tend to be quite brittle.

Invisible repairs

No one finish is typically better than any other. What's really important is that repairs and scratches can be touched up invisibly with both oil-based and spirit-based varnishes. Nitrocellulose lacquer, when applied properly, is a natural, flexible, sprayed-on finish that can be repaired successfully too.

Synthetic varnishes

Low-priced cellos often have a synthetic finish (*i.e.*, polyurethane). This glossy type of finish can be applied very quickly using spray guns, and it's strong, hard, and easy to clean. Being so hard, on the other hand, it may reduce the instrument's sound potential, especially if it has been applied very thickly. Another drawback is that it doesn't allow for invisible repairs.

Shading

Cellos are not always the same color all over. Older instruments may have a lighter patch where the left hand touches the body, for instance. These worn-out patches are sometimes imitated on new cellos. This technique, *shading*, makes instruments look older than they really are.

Checked finish

Older cellos often have a *checked finish*, the varnish being marked with a web of tiny cracks. This effect, also known as *craquelure*, can be imitated by the maker. Yet another way to make an instrument look older is to apply a dark dye to bring out the grain.

Aged to order

Antiquing is a generic name for making a cello look older

than it is, which often raises its price. If you have an instrument custom-built, you can of course ask to have it 'antiqued.' Even minor damage and worn-out spots can be imitated. These aging processes are purely cosmetic.

Flamed wood

The wood of the backs and ribs of many cellos looks like it's been licked by flames. This *flamed, figured,* or *curled wood*

is common on more expensive instruments, but you may also find it in the lowest price range. Whether the wood is plain, or slightly-, medium-, or well-flamed does not relate to its quality or sound potential. On the other hand, beautifully flamed wood has its price: In student and intermediate price ranges the highly-flamed instruments are often the most expensive ones.

A mirrored, flamed back.

Bookmatched

Many flamed backs clearly show that they're made up of two precisely mirrored or *bookmatched* halves (see pages 110–111).

The scroll

Something else to look at is the scroll, which usually has three windings. The center (the *ears*) can stick out more or less, and scrolls are also different when it comes to the *fluting* – the carved grooves in the back. The scroll is sometimes referred to as the signature of the instrument: Experts can tell the maker of a cello by examining the scroll.

ear

The scroll is one of the maker's signatures.

Purfling

The inlaid purfling is not just for decoration. It also prevents cracks at the edge from extending to the *plates* (top and back). Double purfling, a characteristic of the Brescian

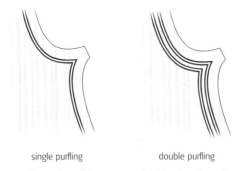

single purfling   double purfling

Purfling usually consists of three or more inlaid strips of wood.

school (see page 117) is rare, but you may come across it. A tip: On very cheap cellos, the purfling is sometimes not inlaid, but painted, or scratched into the wood and dyed.

THE BODY

Generally speaking, a larger body may give you a slightly larger sound. Some instruments may have noticeably wider bodies than others, or just a wider or a slimmer waist (the *C-bout*), and some cellos are slightly shorter or taller.

The ribs

Cellos may vary in their depth too. A relatively shallow instrument, (with low *ribs*), may sound a little thin; a cello that is too deep may have a hollow sound. A cello is always a little deeper at the tail than it is at the top of the body.

String length

If you measure the *string length* (from the nut to the bridge) of a number of instruments you may find differences too. The usual string length is 27.36" (695 mm). When trying out a number of instruments, you may find yourself playing out of tune on some of them. This may be due to a different string length, or to a different *mensur ratio*. More about this can be found in the Glossary (*String length*, page 122). Learning to play an instrument with deviant dimensions in tune usually takes just a little time.

The top

The top is the most important part of a cello. When you play, the strings make the top vibrate, and it is mainly these vibrations that determine the sound of the instrument. This explains why the top is often referred to as the *soundboard*.

Spruce
The top, also known as *table* or *belly*, is almost always made of solid spruce, which has been carved into shape. Spruce is also used for the bass bar and the sound post.

Maple
The back is usually made of one or two carved pieces of solid maple, a heavier and denser kind of wood than spruce. Maple is used for the ribs and the neck as well. One-piece backs are often made of other types of wood, such as willow or poplar, both softer woods, resulting in a slightly softer, warmer sound.

Laminated wood
Cheap cellos may have a laminated back or top, or both, made up of several plies of wood. These plywood plates are very durable and crack-resistant, but they will not make for a rich, musical sound. If you're not sure whether the plates are solid or plywood, check the edges of the plates and the *f*-holes.

Fine grain
Cellists often prefer the top to have a grain that is straight, even, and not too wide, getting gradually finer toward the center of the instrument. Of course, some cellos have a beautiful grain but don't sound good, and there are great instruments with a wide, uneven, or wavy grain as well.

The arching
A top with a lower *arching* will usually help produce a stronger, more powerful and direct sound; a higher arching may contribute to a softer, warmer timbre. Most modern

The back is a little flatter than the top.

cello tops are slightly over an inch high. The back is usually a little flatter.

The channel
A cello with a deep, broad channel will often have a softer sound than an instrument that has only a hint of this 'valley' along the edge.

Flowing lines
You can spend hours looking at cello archings. They all look similar, yet they're all slightly different. What is especially important is that the lines of the arch flow, that there are no flat parts or odd angles, and that the arching isn't too high, too low, or too narrow. The more often you look, the more you'll see.

Thick and thin
Low-cost cellos may have thicker tops or backs, which are easier to make. If they're too thick, the instrument may sound thinnish. Good instruments have *graduated* plates, their exact thickness varying from spot to spot. The top usually varies from about 0.19" in the middle to 0.14" at the edges (4.75–3.5 mm). The back is a little thicker overall.

Hot hide glue
Most better instruments are assembled using animal glue (*hot hide glue*). Joints fixed with this type of glue can be loosened, for example to take the top off for repairs inside the instrument. Also, this type of glue will let go if the wood shrinks or expands as a result of age, or changes in humidity, for instance when winter comes. This prevents the plates from cracking; all the violin maker has to do is to apply new glue. The overhang of the edges warrants that these 'repairs' can be made invisible.

NECK AND FINGERBOARD
The neck and fingerboard affect not only the playability, but also the sound of a cello.

Ebony
Fingerboards are almost always made of ebony. This is a nearly black, extremely hard type of wood. The smoother

and more even the fingerboard, the more easily it plays. Cheap cellos sometimes have fingerboards of softer, light-colored wood, which is often dyed black to make it look like ebony. You can sometimes recognize them by lighter patches or pale spots on the sides.

Wear

After years of use, even the hardest fingerboard will wear, after which it should be reworked or, eventually, replaced (see Chapter 10, *Cello Maintenance*). Incidentally, the use of ebony doesn't guarantee a good fingerboard *per se*: There are cheap, soft types of ebony as well.

Clearance

The fingerboard has a curved top, similar to the top of the bridge. On most fingerboards, the area under the C-string has been flattened. This provides extra clearance for the wide vibrations of this string, preventing it from rattling against the fingerboard. These fingerboards, introduced by the German cellist Bernard Romberg in the mid-nineteenth century, are recognizable by the sharp 'ridge' between the G- and the C-string.

Thick fingers

The grooves in the nut, at the top of the fingerboard, determine the string spacing and the string height at that end. Nuts can be replaced to adjust both string spacing and height. For example, if you have thick fingers, you may prefer a nut with grooves set a little further apart.

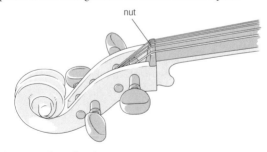

nut

The nut can be replaced.

Feel the neck

Necks are always much lighter in color – a dark neck would soon show worn patches. On more expensive cellos, the wood is usually not varnished but protected with an oil finish. A tip: Feel if the curve of the neck lies nicely in your hand and that there are no odd pits or bumps.

Concave fingerboard

The fingerboard is very slightly concave along its length. This prevents the strings from buzzing when playing in the higher positions.

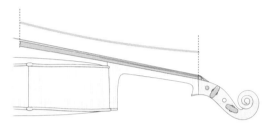

The fingerboard: slightly concave.

Straight

The neck and fingerboard, from scroll to body, should of course be straight. They should also be set exactly in the center line of the cello; and they shouldn't look as though someone has tried to wrench the instrument out of shape. To check, just take a good long look along the fingerboard from the scroll toward the bridge. Also check whether the strings run perfectly straight along the fingerboard, which of course requires a properly installed tailpiece and bridge.

Backwards

The neck of a modern cello is tilted slightly backwards. Before the 1800s, there was a 90-degree angle between the neck and the side of the body. These instruments sounded softer, as the larger neck angle reduced the pressure of the strings on the bridge. Conversely, a smaller neck angle

A smaller neck angle gives a bigger sound.

33

means more pressure on the bridge, which makes the sound bigger, louder, or more radiant.

Baroque cello

The larger neck angle is characteristic of the Baroque cello, which is still used to play music of the Baroque era (c. 1600–1750). The instrument's mellow, gentle sound is also due to a lower bridge, a shorter neck, the use of gut strings, a different bow, and a lower tuning.

STRING HEIGHT

The string height is the distance between the strings and the fingerboard. Having your strings very high above the fingerboard makes it hard work to play. If they are too low, they may rattle. In between, it's largely a matter of taste and the type of strings you're using. A greater string height can give your instrument a slightly clearer, brighter, or more powerful sound.

Room to move

At the nut, the strings are very close to the fingerboard. At the other end, the distance between the fingerboard and the strings is a lot bigger. There, the thick strings are always slightly higher above the fingerboard than the thin ones, because they need more room to move.

The figures

As a rule of thumb, if you use steel core strings, the A-string should be about 0.18"–0.22" (4.5–5.5 mm) above the end of the fingerboard, and the C-string about 0.26"–0.30" (6.5–7.5 mm). Add about 0.04" (1 mm) for gut strings; synthetic core strings are in between.

Too high

If you have a new cello that has not yet been properly adjusted, the strings will probably be too high. Adjusting may involve having the bridge and the nut adapted.

THE BRIDGE

The bridge matters not only for the string height, but also for the sound of the instrument.

Straight

Bridges are a bit slanted at the front and straight at the back. The straight back should be perpendicular to the instrument's top, and the middle of the bridge's feet should be exactly between the notches of the *f*-holes – though some instruments sound better if the bridge is moved forward or backward a tiny bit.

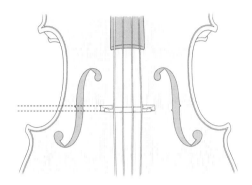

... exactly between the notches of the *f*-holes...

Flecked

Some bridges are plain, while others may be highly flecked or speckled. In itself, this difference tells you nothing about the quality of the wood: Non-flecked (plain), slightly flecked, and highly flecked wood is used for both cheap and expensive bridges. A fine, straight grain is more important.

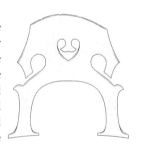

A flecked bridge: cheap or expensive...

(Un)treated

String instrument catalogs often indicate whether bridges are treated or untreated, which refers to the bridges being finished with varnish or oil. Some makers feel that this finish enhances the quality of the bridge; others rather use untreated ones.

Too heavy, too light

Of course you're not going to weigh the bridge when you're choosing a cello, but it's worth knowing that a heavy bridge can muffle the sound slightly, just like a mute (see page 71). A very light bridge may be the culprit if an instrument has a very thin, weak, or uncentered tone. The hardness of the wood also plays a role. A bridge made of harder wood ensures more volume and a stronger, brighter tone.

French and Belgian bridges

Cello bridges come in two basic models. The French type of bridge has shorter legs and longer wings; Belgian bridges, with longer legs, have less mass. Soundwise, French bridges enhance the lower frequencies of the instrument, and they may make the sound a bit mellower. Conversely, you may want to use a Belgian bridge for a brighter, more pronounced sound and a lot of clarity on the D- and A-strings, but the low register may suffer a little.

A French (left) and a Belgian bridge (right).

Blanks

The bridges you find in stores and catalogs are blanks: Bridges always need to be custom-fit to your instrument. There are bridges with moveable feet that automatically adjust to the arch of the top – but even if you prefer this type of bridge, it should be installed by a specialist: Properly fitting a bridge to an instrument involves more than carving the feet (see also page 95).

Too deep

Eventually, the strings will wear into the bridge. If the grooves have become too deep, the strings will be muffled and harder to tune. The string height will be decreased as well, and the strings may break sooner. Ideally, the grooves should be just so deep that two-thirds of the thickness of each string sticks out above the bridge.

Cutting string

The A-string is the one most likely to cut into your bridge. This can be prevented by a plastic sleeve (see page 55) or a piece of vellum (parchment) under the string. Some bridges have a bone or hardwood insert for the same purpose.

A bridge with an ebony inset.

Two at once

The top of the bridge has almost the same curve as the fingerboard. Beginning cellists often prefer a highly-curved bridge: A higher curve reduces the chance of inadvertently bowing two strings instead of one.

Warping bridges

Nearly all bridges warp slightly in time with the pressure of the strings. A cello will produce its best sound only with a straight bridge – so check your bridge from time to time (also see page 94).

Height and tone

The bridge height influences both string height and tone. A slightly higher bridge increases the string tension, which makes the sound a little brighter or stronger. If the bridge is too high, the sound may become a little hollow.

THE SOUND POST

Inside the body, slightly 'behind' the bridge, is the sound post. This thin round spruce stick is not just there for strength: It also has a lot to do with the sound. French violin makers even call it *l'âme*: the *soul* of the instrument.

Position

The sound post must be straight, and long enough to be firmly wedged, but not so long that it pushes the top and the back apart. The exact position is critical too, measured to under a twentieth of an inch.

Adjustment

A violin maker can adjust the timbre of a cello by moving the sound post a fraction. In this way the sound can be made slightly less edgy, or a little brighter, for example. Also, if one string sounds louder or softer than the others, the violin maker can do something about it by repositioning the sound post. You can also try using different strings – but that's another chapter (Chapter 6, to be precise).

PEGS AND FINE TUNERS

You can tune a cello with the wooden tuning pegs at the top. If you play steel strings, you will have to use the fine tuners in the tailpiece as well. Both pegs and fine tuners come in different types and sizes.

Ebony, rosewood, boxwood

Tuning pegs get thicker toward the thumb piece. This tapered shape prevents them from slipping. They are usually made of ebony, which is also used for fingerboards and tailpieces. Rosewood and boxwood are popular too. Rosewood has a reddish-brown color; boxwood is usually yellowish.

Worn grooves

If the wood of the pegs is too soft, the strings will soon wear grooves into them. These grooves, in turn, may damage the strings.

A good fit

Cheap cellos are often hard to tune, or they go out of tune quickly because the pegs are poor in quality or haven't been custom-fit to the instrument properly.

Parisian eyes

Pegs come with various peg head designs, a familiar one being an inverted heart with a ball on top. Another type of decoration is a *Parisian eye*: a small, mother-of-pearl dot with a metal ring around it. A single mother-of-pearl dot is called a (*single*) *eye* or *eyelet*.

Removable pegs

Depending on your posture and the way you hold the cello,

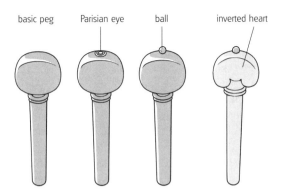

basic peg   Parisian eye   ball   inverted heart

Various tuning-peg designs

the tuning pegs of the C- and G-strings may bother you. To solve that problem, you can have your instrument provided with tuning pegs with a removable thumb piece. Once your strings have been tuned, you simply take out the 'keys.'

Fine tuners   Tipcode CELLO-006

Steel core strings respond so quickly to turning the big tuning pegs, that you need fine tuners to get them at their exact pitches. Usually, these fine tuners are built into the tailpiece. They're also known as *adjusters*, *tuning* or *string adjusters*, *string tuners…*

Too heavy

You can buy fine tuners separately as well, usually at some ten dollars each. A tip: If your cello has a wooden tailpiece,

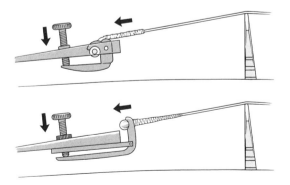

Built-in fine tuners (above) are smaller than the ones available separately (below).

which usually is quite heavy by itself, the added weight of the fine tuners may muffle the sound of your instrument. If so, you may be better off buying a lightweight alloy or synthetic tailpiece with built-in fine tuners.

Geared pegs

Instead of fine tuners, you can get a special type of pegs with a built-in planetary gear system. These 'gear boxes' make both rough and fine tuning possible. Also, these special pegs are easier to operate than traditional pegs, and they don't stick or slip with changes in temperature and humidity.

Metal pegs and tuning machines

As a rarely used alternative there are metal pegs with very thin shafts. Also, some (mainly older) cellos have metal tuning machines similar to the ones used on double basses.

TAILPIECE

Tailpieces, believe it or not, may also influence the sound of your instrument – though you need to have a good instrument and be a good cellist to notice those subtleties. Tailpieces come in various materials and designs, and with or without decoration or built-in fine tuners.

French or Hill

There is a great variety of tailpiece models available. Two examples of well-known basic designs would be the French model, with a very slim upper part, or the Hill model, named after a British manufacturer, with elegant lines and an angular end. Some tailpieces have a Parisian eye or other inlaid decorations.

Parallel

The strings should always run parallel between the bridge and the tailpiece. If not, the tailpiece may be too narrow or too wide for the instrument.

The sound

The tailpiece has roughly the same effect on the sound of the cello as the bridge. A heavy, wooden tailpiece can slightly muffle the sound, making it a little less bright,

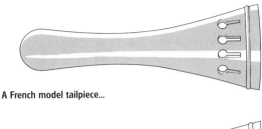

A French model tailpiece...

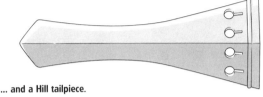

... and a Hill tailpiece.

somewhat similar to what a heavy bridge or a light mute would do. Conversely, a lighter (alloy or synthetic) tailpiece gives a clearer, brighter sound. The sound may become a bit uncentered too – just as with a bridge that is too light.

All together
Of course, these differences are not that obvious. However, the combined mass of a heavy, wooden tailpiece with four big fine tuners can make your instrument sound noticeably duller, especially if the tailpiece is too close to the bridge (see page 95).

Tailpiece loop
Traditionally, the tailpiece loop or *hanger* is made of gut, hence its other name, *tailgut*. There are cellists who feel even this enhances the sound of the instrument, but most tailpieces are attached with an adjustable synthetic cord, which is more reliable and cheaper, or with a steel wire. Gut does have a very attractive look, though, especially on an old instrument.

END PIN
The end pin doesn't do much more than support the instrument. To prevent the height adjustment thumb screw from slipping, the rod may have indentations or a knurled surface. A tip: If the rod has indentations, you may use them to memorize its height setting.

Collar

A cello with a full ebony trim also has an ebony end pin plug, but plugs can be made of other types of wood too. Some have decorations, such as a gold-plated collar around the plug.

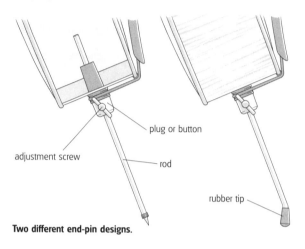

plug or button

adjustment screw

rod

rubber tip

Two different end-pin designs.

Hollow or solid

End pins come with a hollow or a solid rod, the latter simply being a little heavier. Most experts agree that the end pin does not influence the tone of the instrument. However, some players prefer hollow (or solid) rods for sound reasons. Similarly, some favor wooden end pins, which have become quite rare, and others use a modern, light-weight carbon fiber version. Comparing end pins with your ears is usually quite hard, by the way – first, because the differences are so subtle, and second, because end pins are not universal: Replacing them is not simply a matter of pulling one out and putting another one in.

Bent end pin

Players who let their instrument lean very far backwards may benefit from a bent end pin. On some end pins you can even adjust the angle. A less expensive solution is to use a rod with a small bend at the very end.

Rubber tip

The rubber tip at the end of the rod won't keep the instrument from slipping away on all surfaces. If you take the tip off, you will usually see a sharp steel point, which works even better on most wooden surfaces – but of course, you're not supposed to damage the floor you're playing on.

Anchors

To prevent your instrument from sliding away or from damaging the floor or a rug, you may use an end pin anchor. These are available in a wide variety, ranging from simple rubber balls and non-skid discs to holders that can be attached to the front legs of your chair with adjustable straps or cords. They usually cost between ten and twenty-five dollars. The designs that attach to your chair are guaranteed to work on all surfaces. Some players feel that the sound suffers from using an end pin holder; they prefer playing with the steel point stuck into a wooden stage. Other experts state that no one can tell the difference.

Height setting

The best height setting for the end pin depends on many factors, from your height and your posture, to the height of your seat, and the angle at which you hold the cello. Most rods are adjustable up to 20", and they can be replaced by even longer ones.

Cello chairs

Children need a lower seat for optimum posture. Special height-adjustable cello chairs are available, but other height-adjustable chairs and stools may do also – as long as they have a flat or slightly forward-leaning seat.

PLAY-TESTING TIPS

If you try ten cellos in a row, you'll have forgotten what the first one sounded like by the time you try the last. Here are some tips for play-testing instruments.

Take it with you

If you already have a cello, take it with you when you go to choose a new one. Comparing it to different cellos makes it easier to judge what you hear. If you have your own bow, take that with you too. Otherwise, use the best bow available in the store. Using a good bow will give you a better idea of what the different cellos are capable of.

Someone else

If you don't play yourself, or have only just started, you won't know whether an instrument has a poor sound, or whether it's just you. So ask someone who does play to demonstrate the different cellos to you. That someone could also be the dealer, for instance.

By ear

If you ask someone else to play, you can also hear how the instrument sounds from a distance. That sound will be quite different compared to having it right by your ear. Another tip: If you simply can't choose between a few cellos, turn around. Then you won't know which one is being played, so you'll really be choosing by ear only. You won't see the price, the finish, the brand name, or the age anymore. Sometimes musicians choose much cheaper instruments than they expected to by ear – but it may be the other way around too.

Very different

To get an idea of how cellos sound in the room you're in, you may start by playing two very different cellos, one with a bright sound, and one with a mellow, dark sound. Knowing these extremes also can make your search easier.

Three by three

First, make a rough selection of the instruments you like on first hearing. Take three of them, and compare them with one another. Replace the one you like least by another cello from your rough selection. Compare the three again – and so on.

Something simple

If you have a lot of cellos to choose from, it's often easier if you only play briefly on each one. Play something simple, so that you can concentrate on the instrument, rather than on what you play. Even a scale will do. When you have a few cellos left, and you really need to choose, you'll probably want to play longer and more demanding pieces so that you can get to know the instruments better.

String by string

You can also compare cellos string by string and note by

note. How do the open strings sound, and how do they sound in the highest positions? Is there a good balance between the volume of the strings in all positions? How do the strings sound when you pluck them, or when you play long notes?

Same pitch, same strings

The cellos that you are comparing must be tuned properly and to the same pitch. Otherwise, one instrument might sound a little warmer than the others, say, just because it is tuned a bit lower. For similar reasons, the cellos you are judging should all have the same or similar strings. If not, you will be comparing strings instead of cellos.

LISTENING TIPS

Here are some things to listen for when play-testing cellos.

Projection and volume

Some cellos will always sound very soft or weak, however energetically you play them. In an orchestra with one such instrument, no one will be able to hear you. Other cellos can be heard at a fair distance too, even if you play very softly. A cello like that has good *projection*. Of course, cellos also differ in the volume level they can produce: Some just sound louder than others.

Same note, different timbre

The A-string not only sounds higher than the other strings, it also sounds different. If you play an A first on the open A-string, and then play the same pitch on the D- and G-strings, you'll hear that very same pitch with three very different timbres. Cellists usually want their low strings to sound warm and dark, and their higher strings brilliant and singing brightly, all within a musical balance: The differences from string to string should not be like going from one instrument to another.

Response and depth of sound

A cello should have a good response, even when you play very softly. If not, the instrument will be hard to play; it will make you really work for each note. If a cello has a poor response, it takes a little while before the tone is really 'there.' The C-string is the most critical one when it comes to response, as it's so heavy. This string is also most likely to lack depth of sound, followed by its neighbor, the G.

Uncentered tone

On some cellos, the sound never seems to gel; these instruments lack foundation, producing an uncentered, weak tone. Both a slow response and an uncentered tone can also stem from the strings, the bow, the rosin, or – sadly – yourself.

Dynamics and colors

A cello should be able to sound just as loud or soft as you play. If it does, it has good dynamics. If it doesn't, your performance will always be a bit shallow. The instrument should also allow you to produce different timbres or 'colors.' One example: If you play a little closer to the fingerboard, the sound is supposed to become noticeably rounder than if you play close to the bridge (*sul ponticello*). Ideally, the instrument should sound good both ways, leaving you plenty of room to color the sound.

Sound and words

Apart from that, sound is mostly a matter of personal preference. Bear in mind that when two people listen to the same instrument, they'll probably use different words to describe what they hear. What one finds harsh or edgy (in other words, unpleasant), another may describe as bright and clear (in other words, pleasant), and what's warm to one ear sounds dull to another. It all depends on what you do and do not like – and how you put that into words.

Rich

The better an instrument is, the richer it sounds. Richer means a beautiful, resonant, full-throated tone; it means there's more of everything; and it means that the cello allows for producing a wide variety of tonal colors: mellow and vivid, subdued and bright, sad and happy…

Poor

Some words associated with poorer-sounding instruments are nasal (as if it has a cold), hollow (like you're playing in a bathroom), thin (as if it were a miniature instrument), or dull (as if there were a blanket over it) – and everybody has more or less the same idea of what those words mean.

USED CELLOS

When you go to buy a used instrument, there are a few extra things you should remember.

Repairs

No matter what's broken, a decent cello can almost always be fixed. Of course, if you decide to buy an instrument that needs some work, you need to know what it's going to cost first. Some types of damage are easy to see, other kinds only an expert will spot. Also, you need to be an expert to judge things like how well a cello has been repaired. If in doubt, take a cello for appraisal first (see also page 23).

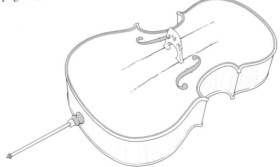

Major damage: cracks in the sound post and bass bar areas.

Used-instrument checks

Here are some things to check when buying a secondhand instrument. A complete list would be too long for this book.

- **Varnish wears**. One place to check is where your left hand touches the body. If the varnish has completely gone, you may need to have something done about it.
- If the type of varnish allows for it, it is usually **touched up** after repairs (see page 27). See if this has been done properly.
- Check **the edges**: This is where the instruments gets bumped most often. Repairing damaged edges can cost a lot of money.

- Cracks in the top or the back always run lengthwise. Cracks by **the sound post and the bass bar** are often hard to see and even harder to repair.
- Other places to check for cracks include **the shoulder of the neck and the cheeks** (sides) of the pegbox near the pegs.
- If **the tuning pegs** are pushed very far into the pegbox, sticking way out at the other end, they may need to be replaced, and the holes may need to be rebushed – which is quite an expensive job.
- Glue can come loose, along the edges for instance, or at the neck. To discover **loose glue joints** you can play the instrument or gently tap it, all around the body.

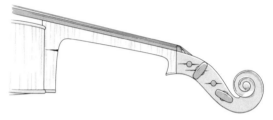

Cracks in the cheeks and the shoulder of the neck.

Woodworm

Woodworm burrows into wood and leaves narrow tunnels. This can be very serious, especially if it has been at work in the top or the back. You won't find woodworm in a cello that has always been played: This particular animal doesn't like music. If you want to know whether it's still around, lay the instrument on a piece of black cardboard overnight. If there's sawdust on the cardboard the next day, the cello has tenants.

6. GOOD STRINGS

The strings you use determine your sound to a great extent. You can choose between dozens of different types of strings, with different core materials and windings. Every type of string has its own timbre, some types of strings are easier to play than others, and some sound better on one cello than on another.

Cello strings can last a long time – up to a year, or even longer. It does help if they are fitted properly and kept clean. For more information on replacing strings and keeping them in good condition, go to Chapter 10, *Cello Maintenance.*

Steel, gut, synthetic
There are three main types of strings. Today, most cellists use strings with a steel core. Originally, cellos had gut strings, which sound a lot warmer and darker. Strings with a synthetic core – the third type – have a sound in between the other two.

Winding
Almost all cello strings are wound with ultra-thin metal ribbon. If not, they would have to be very thick in order to produce the desired pitches – and thick strings do not respond very well. The material of the ribbon is very important to the way the strings sound, play, and respond.

... wound with ultra-thin
metal ribbon.

Important

Again, strings are very important for how you sound and play. Actually, the difference between using cheap and expensive strings is often much bigger than the difference between a cheaper and a more expensive cello.

Experiment

So, if you can afford it, try to experiment with different types of strings. When you do, please note that changing from steel to synthetic or gut strings will require you to adapt your technique, which may require extra lessons from a teacher who plays those types of strings. Your instrument will probably need to be adapted too (see page 93).

STEEL STRINGS

Strings with a steel core offer a clear, bright, powerful sound and an immediate response. Also, they're very reliable and they last a long time, typically from six months to a year, or even longer.

The core

Steel strings come in two basic variations: with a solid core, and with a core made up of a number of very thin steel strands. Solid or full-core strings have the brightest sound. Multi-strand or spiral-core strings are more flexible, and produce a darker, fuller tone.

Combinations

Many cellists combine both types on their instrument. They often use solid-core A- and D-strings for radiant, bright highs, and multi-strand G- and C-strings for warm, full-sounding lows. Others combine synthetic and steel strings, for example (see below). Such 'custom sets' are readily available from some stores, but you can make up your own combination as well, of course.

The price

Most cheap cellos have steel strings, as they are relatively low-priced. A set of four is available for around seventy-five dollars, and sometimes even less. Professional-quality steel strings may easily cost twice as much, and there are C-strings that list for more than a hundred dollars.

GUT STRINGS

The first cellos had sheep gut strings. Some professional musicians still feel that this is the only type of string that can really reveal the instrument's beauty.

Sound

The sound of gut strings is often described as mellow, warm, and rich. They allow for great variation in color and inflection – which in turn demands a good cellist, and a good cello too. Baroque music (see page 34), requiring a warm, gentle type of sound, is often played using gut strings. These are sometimes wound with round wire (round wound), like in the Baroque era, rather than with a flat ribbon. Some Baroque players use unwound (*plain*) D- and A-strings.

A few hours

Contrary to steel strings, gut strings need to be broken in: It takes a few hours of playing to get them to develop their full sound. As they stretch a fair bit when new, you'll have to tune gut strings quite often at first. Additional tuning is also required as gut strings detune with changes in temperature or humidity.

Expensive

A set of gut strings easily costs a hundred to two hundred dollars, but they're available for less as well. What adds to their price is that they don't last as long as other types of strings. Many cellists use a gut A-string only, combined with three synthetic-core strings.

SYNTHETIC STRINGS

Synthetic-core strings could be considered 'in between' gut and steel, in terms of sound, life expectancy, and price. A set of four typically costs a hundred dollars or more.

Sound

As there's a large variety in synthetic-core materials and windings, there's a large variety in sound too. Generally speaking, the sound is close to that of gut strings, though a bit brighter and louder. Synthetic strings are more reliable and less expensive, and they last longer. Compared to steel strings they sound noticeably warmer – or less hard and bright…

Best of both worlds
Synthetic-core strings are often combined with other types of strings. One popular combination is to use synthetic-core strings for the C and the G, and steel for the other two.

Breaking them in
Just like gut strings, synthetic-core strings may start to sound their best only after they are played for a few hours. When they are brand-new, they can sound a little raw or harsh. Also, they're a bit stretchy when new, so they will require some additional tuning, and a bit of time to settle in.

WINDINGS
String manufacturers use various types of windings, each with its own effect on the strings' sound and playability. To create a particular balance between the four strings, they may even use different winding materials within one set, and strings can also have more than one winding.

Nickel or chrome
Generally speaking, a nickel winding will make for a rather soft, sweet, or warm sound. Chromium or chrome-alloy windings, on the other hand, add brightness to the sound and enhance the projection of the instrument.

Silver, aluminum, and tungsten
A silver winding adds warmth and power to the lower strings. Silver-wound lower strings are often combined with aluminum-wound treble strings, the lighter metal providing extra clarity in the higher ranges. Tungsten is used instead of or in combination with silver. This dense material allows for even thinner low strings, which enhances their response. Tungsten may also help to fight wolf tones (see page 74).

More
There are many more materials used to wind strings, including copper, titanium, and silver mixed with gold. If you are looking for a particular sound, a good salesperson or violin maker will be able to help you with your choice.

But if youwant to be really sure, you'll need to try out different strings for yourself.

Discolor
Depending on your perspiration and chemical makeup, silver and aluminum windings may discolor very fast. If this happens, the best you can do is experiment with other types of windings.

LOUD OR SOFT
Synthetic and steel strings often come in several varieties: *dolce* (soft), *medium*, and *forte* (strong), for instance. You may also see German descriptions like *weich* (soft) and *stark* (strong). Forte strings, also indicated as *orchestra* or *solo*, are heavier than dolce strings.

Different tensions
Some string manufacturers describe their strings by their tension, marketing low-, medium-, and high-tension strings. The higher the tension, the heavier the string's gauge. High-tension strings take a little more effort to play and they respond slower than low-tension versions, but their brighter, stronger sound enhances the projection of your instrument. Medium strings are the most commonly used. Low-tension strings are often recommended for old instruments.

Too much tension
Choosing the right type of strings is not just down to the sound or playability: Using forte strings may work great on one cello, but their higher tension may actually reduce the sound on another instrument.

Colors
To indicate the different types of strings, manufacturers use colored thread at one of the string's ends. At the other end, the string's pitch is marked with another color, to prevent you from putting the D-string where the A-string should be, for example.

Confusing
Unfortunately, these color codes are not standardized, so

the same color may mean one thing for one make and something else for the next. Likewise, there's no consistency in what (string type, string pitch) is indicated at which end of the string. Confusing…

Same make and series
A tip: If the strings on a cello are of the same make and series, you will see four different colors (indicating the pitch of each string) at one end, and only one color (indicating the series or type of strings) at the other.

Mixed up
If this is not so, there's a fair chance that strings are of different brands, series, or tensions – assembled either on purpose or inadvertently. If the strings sound good together, that's no problem. If you want to know which strings are fitted to your instrument, ask an expert, who can tell from the color codes.

Thick or thin
Gut strings come in different gauges. Heavier-gauge strings take more effort to play. They sound noticeably fuller, louder, and clearer; and they don't respond as easily as thinner strings.

Inches and millimeters
If you want to know exactly how thick a gut string is in inches, divide its gauge by 500 (*e.g.*, a 14 is $14 \div 500 = 0.028"$). To get millimeters, divide the gauge by 20.

String height
If you fit higher-tension strings on your instrument, those strings may end up further from the fingerboard. Conversely, lower-tension strings can decrease the instrument's string height, as they reduce the tension on the neck. Adjusting string height is a job for a professional.

AND MORE
If you're putting new strings on your cello, you can list their details on pages 129–130 of this book. Then you'll be able to buy the same type again if you like them, or avoid them if you don't. This can be especially helpful if you mix

and match string sets yourself. The more you know about the strings you use, the better you'll be able to adjust the sound of your instrument to your taste.

How long

How long cello strings last depends on many things – on how often you play, of course, but also on the core material of the strings and the type of winding, and on how well you keep your strings clean (see Chapter 10, *Cello Maintenance*). A tip: If the tension on a string is suddenly released (for example, because of an ill-fitting tuning peg or a sudden change in air humidity; see page 97), the winding may be damaged or the string may break as you bring it back to pitch.

A year

If you have steel strings and you play for a few hours a week, you might try fitting new strings after a year or so. If you hear the difference straightaway, try replacing the new set a couple of months earlier. If you can't hear any difference after a year, you may wait longer before replacing your strings next time. Steel strings usually last longer then synthetic strings. Gut strings wear out the quickest.

Short and dull

When should you replace your strings? When plucking them only produces a short, dull tone, they are wearing out. If they become discolored, you're also better off replacing them. Note, however, that silver-wound and aluminum-wound strings may still sound fine long after they have begun to discolor.

Damaged windings

A damaged winding often renders a string unplayable. You can prevent this from happening by making sure the grooves in the bridge and nut are wide enough for the strings you use (have them checked when you change to thicker strings), and by 'lubricating' the grooves from time to time by rubbing them with a soft lead pencil point.

Sleeves

Some strings come with short sleeves that are designed to protect the winding at the bridge. If you choose to use them, make sure that most of the sleeve is on the side of the tailpiece; otherwise it will muffle the sound too much. If muffling an overly bright string is what you want to do, there are more effective devices available (see page 73).

Parchment

To prevent the thin A-string from cutting into the bridge, some bridges have an ebony or bone insert at that point, and violin makers often glue a tiny piece of vellum (parchment) under the string.

Fractional sizes

Fractional-sized strings are available for smaller instruments. Regular strings will typically provide insufficient tension, resulting in a weak tone and possible string breakage. The choice in fractional-sized strings is quite limited; it's usually best to rely on the teacher's experience in this matter. Incidentally, some teachers happen to prefer certain types or regular strings on small cellos.

String brands

Choosing the right strings can also be hard because of the wide selection that is available. There are quite a number of string brands on the market. Most of them offer various types of cello and other strings, and some market rosins, other accessories or even instruments as well. D'Addario, Pirastro, Super-Sensitive, and Thomastik are some of the bigger companies. Other brands are Corelli, Jargar, Larsen, and Dogal, Meisel, Pinnacle, Prim, Pyramid, Savarez, Stellar, Supreme, and Syntha-Core. Some of these names are brand names only, being produced by another company.

7. BOWS AND ROSINS

You'll only get the very best from your cello if you have a bow that suits your instrument as well as your style of playing and the music you play. A chapter about brazil-wood and pernambuco, synthetic bows, frogs, ferrules, horsehair or synthetic hair, weight and balance, and rosin.

The stick of the bow can be made of wood or a synthetic material, with wood still being the most popular choice. Most cheaper wooden bows use brazilwood; more expensive bows are made of pernambuco.

Brazil or pernambuco

Expect to pay two to four hundred dollars for a decent brazilwood bow – but they're available for much less too. If you pay more, you'll probably get a bow with a stick made of pernambuco, a slightly reddish type of wood. Pernambuco bows can last more than a hundred years without losing their elasticity.

Four hundred

So, for around four hundred dollars you can buy an 'expensive' brazilwood bow or an affordable pernambuco one. If two bows cost the same, choose the one that suits you and your instrument best – whichever type of wood the bow is made of. Snakewood, a dense, expensive type of wood that derives its name from its snakeskin look, is mainly used for special Baroque bows.

Synthetic bows

Some bows have a synthetic stick – carbon fiber or

fiberglass, for example. The cheapest models, available for fifty dollars or less, are designed mainly for children. They're very durable and don't need much care or attention. Professional synthetic bows are also available, and they can cost thousands of dollars.

Synthetic hair
The very cheapest bows often come with synthetic hair. This provides less grip than the traditional horsehair, and it'll never make the instrument sound its best.

Bleaching
Some manufacturers bleach the bow hair to make it look bright and white all over. However, bleaching reduces the durability of the hair.

The mountings
A bow's *mountings* are its metal parts, such as the screw button, the *back plate* of the frog, and the *ferrule* or *D-ring*, where the bow hair enters the frog. The material used for the mounting very roughly indicates the price range and quality of the bow.

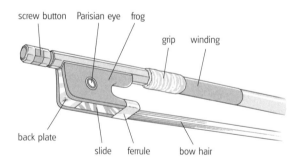

Silver, gold, and nickel silver
Silver-mounted bows usually start at around five hundred dollars, and gold-mounted bows (rare, but they are around) may easily cost five times as much. Most cheaper bows have nickel silver mountings. Contrary to what you might expect, nickel silver does not contain silver.

Full-lined
The frog in the picture above is a *full-lined frog*. A *half-lined*

frog, usually found on cheaper bows, does not have the back plate behind the *slide* or extending underneath to the slide. (The slide is the part at the bottom of the frog.)

CLOSE UP

Of course, there is more to a bow than the type of wood used and the mountings – the shape of the stick, for one thing, and the decorations on and around the frog.

Eight-sided or round

The stick, which gets gradually thinner from the frog to the head, can be round or octagonal (eight-sided). Some cellists feel that octagonal sticks make a bow play better, as they may be a little stiffer or more stable than round sticks.

A little more

A bow with an octagonal stick, *bow stick*, or *shaft* usually costs a little more than one with a round stick – not necessarily because it's better, but simply because it takes more work to make one.

Frog

On better bows, the frog is usually made of ebony, and sometimes of horn or (mammoth) ivory. Cheap bows often have plastic frogs. Most slides have a mother-of-pearl finish. The frog itself is often decorated with single or Parisian eyes. Intricately carved and decorated models are also available.

Screw buttons

Screw buttons, also known as *end screws* or *adjusters* come in two- and three-part versions (*i.e.*, silver-ebony, and silver-ebony-silver, respectively). Some have a single or a Parisian eye on each of its eight sides.

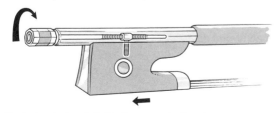

Tensioning the bow hair: The frog moves backward.

Branded name

Usually the name of the bow maker or the bow's brand is literally branded into the stick, just above the frog.

Bow grip

The leather bow grip or *thumb grip* may be a little thinner on one stick than the next, and it may have tiny 'ventilation holes.' Instead of leather, vinyl is sometimes used on less expensive bows. This may feel a little sticky when you play. If the bow grip feels too thin, you can install a thumb cushion, which simply slides over it. If it's too thick, it's best to ask your violin maker or technician to replace it. ·

Winding or lapping

Silver thread is usually used for the winding or *lapping*. Some bows have a silk winding or synthetic imitation baleen windings in one or two colors. The use of real baleen (whalebone) has been banned.

Face

In the past, the protective *face* at the other end of the stick was often made of ivory. Today, bow makers use a synthetic material, metal, or bone.

CHOOSING BOWS

When given the choice between a great instrument and a decent bow, or a decent instrument and a great bow, most professional cellists go for the latter combination. Some cellists even say your bow should cost as much as your cello. Others say half as much, or a quarter – so that's not much help. Your best bow is the one you feel most comfortable with and that helps you to make your instrument sound its best, for a price you can afford.

The best bow?

Which bow suits you best depends on both your bowing technique and on the music you are playing. A bow must suit your instrument too, and the strings you are using – so always try out bows with your own cello.

More expensive

As with cellos, a more expensive bow is not always better,

and an antique bow will often cost a lot more than an equally good new one (see Chapter 4). You can also get lucky and find a great bow for a bargain price. Even top cellists sometimes have a 'cheap' bow in their collection because it happens to be perfect for certain pieces of music.

Suit the music

Again, the bow should suit the style of music you play. That's why cellists often have a variety of bows. Some are better for a bright, clear tone; others are preferable when the music requires a mellow timbre.

Three by three

After you've tried out ten bows in a row, you'll have forgotten what the first one sounded and played like – just like cellos. It's often easier if you concentrate on, say, three bows, after a first rough selection. Reject the one you like least, then take another one to compare the other two with. And so on. First play short, simple pieces, or even just scales, and play longer pieces when you have only a few bows left to choose from.

Hair tension

When comparing bows, take the hair tension into account. The 'best' tension may vary per bow, depending on the elasticity of the stick and your personal preference, among other things.

Starting point

As a starting point, you may want to check the distance between the middle of the stick and the hair. If this is about 0.4" (1 cm), the tension will usually be about right – unless the stick has a deviant taper, for one thing.

Different per bow

Turning the screw button the same number of times for each stick isn't a good starting point, as this will probably result in very different hair tensions per bow. A tip: The number of times you turn the adjustment screw may vary on your own bow too from time to time, depending on humidity and temperature. When the air is very dry, the stick will be slightly stiffer, so you'll need to put less tension on the bow hair, and vice versa.

What to play

Of course, the best test for any bow is to play the music you intend to use it for. Try out all the bowing styles you know. Play slowly, fast, loudly, and softly, play *staccato* and *legato*, and keep listening and feeling how the bow performs. Some bows respond better to the way you play and to where exactly you bow the strings than other models – again, just like cellos.

Sound

A different bow will make you sound different, just like another instrument. In fact, there are even small differences between every two 'identical' bows. These nuances will often come out best if you play slow phrases, and you'll hear more of them when you play more expensive equipment.

Curved   Tipcode CELLO-007

A bow should be curved so that the hair, when slack, just touches the middle of the stick. If the stick is more curved than that, the hair may touch it when playing. Such a bow may also feel a little restless or jumpy. A bow that is too straight, on the other hand, may be sluggish. Looking on the bright side, you could also say that a more curved bow is good for *spiccato* (in which the bow bounces lightly off the strings), while a fairly straight bow would be better for slower phrases. But then, a really good bow should allow you to play anything…

Flexibility   Tipcode CELLO-008

To check the flexibility of a bow, rest its face on a table and gently push it downward with your forefinger in the playing position. A very flexible bow can make it difficult to play fast pieces, but it may have a better tone than a stiffer model. Playing may be easier with a stiffer bow, but producing a good, long tone may become trickier. And again, a good bow should allow you to play anything you can. A tip: There are synthetic bows whose flexibility can be adjusted to match your technique or the music you play.

Weight

A full-sized bow usually weighs between 2.2 and 2.4 ounces (78–85 grams); usually, a bow weight of about 2.3 ounces is recommended. If you're looking for a full-bodied sound, you may want to find a relatively heavy bow. Lighter bows are better suited for a lighter sound. If a bow is too light, it won't make the strings vibrate enough and you won't produce much sound at all.

Small difference
Even the smallest weight differences can influence how you sound and play – and some cellists can spot the tiniest weight differences between two bows.

Balance
The heavier a bow is at the head end, the heavier it will feel. A top-heavy stick may be easier to guide. A stick with the weight further back feels lighter, but you have to guide it more. To compare bow balances, you can carefully balance them on your forefinger at about 9–9.5" from the end of the stick (not including the screw button). A bow's balance can be adapted by using more or less thread for the winding, for example, or even by making the tip heavier.

Response
With some bows, the tone builds up very gently and gradually; with others the strings respond very quickly. To check the response of a bow, play lots of short notes on the lowest strings. Most cellists like to have a bow with an even response – in other words, a bow that produces the same response from the strings in the middle, near the head, and near the frog.

In line
Look along the back of the bow, from the frog, to check that it is straight. Just like a cello neck, the bow must not look as though someone has tried to wrench it out of shape.

Used bows
A few tips if you're planning to buy a used bow:
- If the hair is overstretched, a bow will feel very sluggish. The solution is to have the bow **rehaired** (see page 88).
- Another problem with overstretched bow hair is that the frog needs to be shifted very far back. This changes the **balance of the stick**.

- A bow can **lose some of its curve** or *camber* over the years. It may be possible to restore the curve, but be sure you know whether your bow is worth the expense.
- What Stradivarius is to the cello, **François Tourte** (France, 1747–1835) is to the bow. If you find his name on a bow, it probably won't be a real Tourte, as they easily fetch over fifty thousand dollars.

Brands

A few well-known bow brand names are Arcos Brasil, Ary-France, Dörfler, Höfner, Müller, Paesold, Seifert, Student Arpège, Roger, Werner, and W.R. Schuster. Low-cost synthetic bows are made by Glasser and P&H, amongst other companies; Berg, Coda, and Spiccato make more expensive and professional synthetic bows too.

Workshop and master bows

There are also dozens of small bow workshops worldwide, especially in Germany and France, where bows of around three hundred dollars or more are made. Bows by independent makers, who work alone, start at around a thousand dollars, going up to ten thousand dollars and more. If a bow doesn't have a brand name at all, it's likely to be a very cheap one.

ROSIN

Rosin makes the bow hair slightly sticky so it can properly 'grab' the strings and make them vibrate. When you play a string, the rosin makes it stick to the bow hair – until the tension gets too high as you move the bow along. At that point, the bow hair lets the string slip for a split second. This *stick-slip motion* is what makes the string vibrate.

Many stories

Cellists often use the same type of rosin for years – but experimenting a bit can't hurt. A tip in advance: There are many stories about the differences and similarities of rosins, usually contradicting one another. Trying rosins out yourself is the best thing you can do.

Hard

Each rosin cake comes wrapped in a cloth or in a box so

you're less likely to touch it. It's not only sticky, but also quite hard. As a rule, it will easily last you a year or longer, unless you drop it: Being as hard as it is, there's a good chance it'll break.

Light and dark

Many brands sell rosins in two colors, at the same price: a light, honey-like color, and a darker color, almost like licorice. You often read that light rosins are harder and less sticky (so you should use these in the summer, when the higher temperature will make them softer), and vice versa. This may be true of some brands – but it can be the other way around just as well. Often, only the color is different. When you start playing, that difference vanishes as well: Rosin dust is always white.

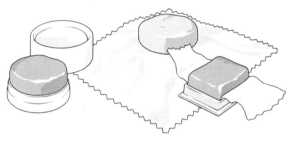

Rosin is sold in cloths and boxes, rectangular or round blocks, and in various colors.

Harder and softer

The rosin of one brand may be harder than that of another, and some brands sell rosin in different hardnesses. You may be able to feel the difference between the softer and harder types by pressing your fingernail into them.

The best rosin?

Even experts don't agree on which rosin to choose. A few examples of their differing opinions? Softer rosin makes your strings respond better, but because it is stickier, it's more likely to produce unwanted noises. You are less likely to get those unwanted noises if you use steel strings. On the other hand, rosin developed for steel strings is often harder than rosin designed for gut strings, supposedly because gut strings don't respond properly if you use a very hard rosin...

Loud music, hard rosin?

Some experts – cellists as well as rosin makers – say that harder rosins are especially suitable for louder music, or when a fast response is required, or when the music you play requires a lot of bow pressure. However, other experts recommend harder types of rosin for quiet pieces; being less sticky, they would produce less unwanted noise.

Sticky

An extra-sticky rosin tends to produce less dust, so less gets onto your cello. What's more, you won't need to apply as much pressure on your bow. On the other hand, this type of rosin is more likely to clog up your bow hair, which will then have to be cleaned more often. Some more expensive rosins, having finer particles, are said to produce more – and finer – dust.

Barely noticeable

Many experts believe the biggest difference between most rosins is the amount of dust they produce during application and just afterwards: Once you are playing, the difference between the various rosins is often barely noticeable, or not at all. Most experts agree that this is even more true if you use a student or intermediate bow.

Gold and silver

Rosins often cost between five and fifteen dollars, including varieties that contain gold or silver particles. The precious metal is said to add clarity and brightness to the sound – although not all cellists can tell the difference.

Trial and error

If you buy a different bow, you may need a different rosin to do it justice; it's the same story if you start using different strings. Unfortunately, choosing the right rosin remains a matter of trial and error. Try out a different type once in a while, just to hear and feel what happens. You may not know what you're missing if you don't.

For hours

Trying out rosins is a slow process: The old rosin will still be effective for several hours of playing after you've applied a new rosin. That's why cellists who use different rosins for different styles of music also have a different bow for each type of rosin – or a different type of rosin for each bow...

The same name

Some manufacturers make it easy for you by giving their different types of rosin the same names as their strings. This can be a good starting point when choosing your rosin. It's also true that the very same rosin is sometimes sold in different packagings with different labels, and different prices, each with their own description!

Cello, violin, viola

One more example of the range of opinions on this subject is that some manufacturers sell different rosins for cello, violin, and viola, while others simply make one rosin for all three instruments.

Allergic?

If you're allergic to traditional rosin, try one of the hypo-allergenic rosins available, or try a rosin that produces less dust.

8. ACCESSORIES

If you buy just a cello, rather than a complete outfit, you'll need to invest in a gig bag or a case. Other accessories for cellists are cello stands, mutes, and devices to suppress the stuttering sound of a wolf tone.

Cello bags and cases are available in a wide variety of styles, the most expensive case easily costing twenty times as much as the cheapest bag. Bags are usually easier to carry around than cases; they weigh less and they're softer. Besides, most bags come with adjustable, padded backpack straps. On the other hand, a good case offers better protection against harder blows.

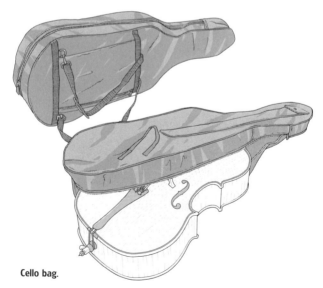

Cello bag.

Cello bags

The cheapest cello bags are available for about forty dollars, but you may also find bags that cost four times as much. The price depends, among other things, on the padding (from none at all to an inch or more) and the quality of the bag itself. For example, 600 Denier nylon is denser and stronger than 420 Denier nylon.

Pockets

Cello bags usually have pockets for your bow and strings, and possibly for other accessories or sheet music. A tip: Always take the bow out before unpacking the cello. This prevents damaging the bow. Another tip: To keep the inside of the bow pocket clean from rosin, put your bow in a separate, washable cotton liner bag.

Cases

Most cello cases have a hard shell made of plywood, fiberglass or a synthetic material. To resist moisture, wooden shells are usually covered with vinyl, leather, or nylon or cordura cloth. Prices range from about three to eight hundred dollars and more. A good case will absorb a shock if it falls, and it's sturdy enough to resist being

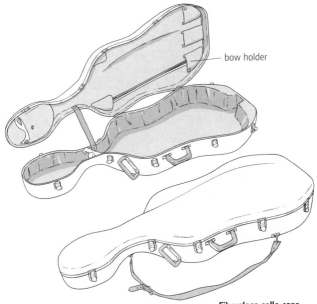

bow holder

Fiberglass cello case.

crushed if something heavy falls on it. The cheapest cases, their cores being less strong, may not offer enough protection.

Inside

A padded, plush-lined interior absorbs shocks and prevent scratches. The padding tends to be thicker in more expensive cases. If a choice between a velour or a velvet lining is offered, the latter will cost a little extra.

Suspension cases

In many cases, the instrument is suspended: The bottom is recessed at the back and the scroll of the instrument.

Protective cloth

Covering the instrument with a cloth before closing the case offers extra protection against damage and dirt from the bow(s). Some cases come with a cloth or a foam pad for that purpose.

Bow holders

The inside of the lid usually has holders for two bows. A tip: Always put the bows in with their hair facing outwards. Separate bow cases are also available, for one or more bows.

Case covers

To prevent your instrument from getting wet when it rains, the case should close properly. For extra protection you may want to invest in a separate case cover. Covers are available with or without extra padding and sheet music pockets.

Locks and hinges

Most cases are lockable. This is mainly to ensure that the catches cannot open by accident – for instance, if you drop your case – so make it a habit to always lock them. When choosing a case, check the locks, hinges, handles, and carrying straps carefully: Usually, these are the weak spots.

Handles, wheels, and feet

Cases and bags often have two or even three handles, making it easier to take the instrument out of a car, for example. Some cases and bags come with (optional) wheels.

It's advisable to use these on even, smooth floors only. To protect the case or bag from wear, it may have rubber or metal feet on the bottom and the sides.

Hygrometer
Cellos are particularly sensitive to very dry air. Some of the more expensive cases available have a built-in hygrometer, so you can check humidity at any time (see page 97).

Cello stands
It's best to keep your instrument in its case or bag when you're not playing. For short breaks, however, it may be easier to place it on a cello stand, rather than lay the instrument on the floor or put it back in its case. Collapsible cello stands, available for around fifty dollars, usually have a holder for the bow too. A warning: The rubber pads on some stands may leave imprints in the varnish, especially in warm weather. As an alternative, there are padded, box-shaped stands – but you can't take these along as you travel.

Another tip: If you don't use a stand and you need to lay your cello down for a minute, always put it on its side – never on its back or top. Rugs can damage your cello, though, for instance as it catches an edge.

A cello stand.

MUTES
If you place a *mute* on the bridge of your instrument, the sound becomes softer, mellower, or warmer: Mutes muffle some of the higher frequencies of the sound. If the composer wants you to use a mute, the score will show the instruction 'with mute' in Italian: *con sordino*. Practice mutes (see page 16) muffle the sound a lot more than regular mutes do.

Bigger and heavier

As discussed on pages 35–36, a heavy bridge may slightly muffle the sound of your instrument. A mute works the same way, basically: You make the bridge heavier by sliding a mute onto it. This extra mass absorbs a part of the vibrations of the bridge, so fewer vibrations are transferred to the body. The bigger or heavier a mute is, the more it will muffle the sound.

Clothing pin

Want to try this out? Very carefully attach a wooden clothing pin to the bridge of your cello, and you'll hear that the sound will be muffled slightly. If you attach

Tourte model

another clothing pin, doubling the added mass, the muffling effect will be even stronger.

Hill model

Variety

Mutes come in rubber, metal, or wood, and in a wide variety of models. Most mutes are very affordable, often costing between five and fifteen dollars.

Detachable or slide-on

The most basic mute, a three-pronged model, looks like a short, thick comb. You put it onto your cello bridge only when you need it. Another type, the fixed mute or slide-on mute, stays attached to the instrument. If you don't need it, you slide it over the strings to the tailpiece. Slide-on mutes come in rubber (*i.e.*, the Tourte model) and wire versions.

wire mute

ebony mute

Various mutes, some looking like short, thick combs...

Which one?

Slide-on mutes are especially easy in pieces where you have to change quickly between playing with and without a mute. There are some cellists who prefer never to use them because, even when they are near the tailpiece, they could muffle the sound (though you're unlikely to hear the difference), or because they might vibrate along with the strings. Others thoroughly dislike clip-on mutes, because they're easy to lose…

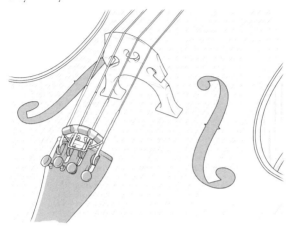

A slide-on wire mute at the tailpiece…

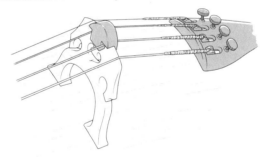

… and a rubber slide-on mute on the bridge.

A tiny bit

A wire mute can be used to make your sound just a tiny bit sweeter. To do so, slide it to a position somewhere between the bridge and the tailpiece. The closer you get to the bridge, the stronger the muffling effect. You can also offset a wire mute diagonally, so that it muffles the high strings more than the low ones, or the other way around.

Tone filter

To slightly mute one or more strings, you can also attach a rubber sleeve around them, at the bridge. An even faster solution is to use a small rubber disc, known as a *tone filter*, which can be put between the string and the bridge without removing the string.

Take it off
Always remove the mute from your instrument before packing it up. If you don't, your cello could get damaged. Small mutes can stay put.

WOLF TONES
Many good cellos are plagued by *wolf tones*: At a certain pitch, the sound seems to stutter, or howl, like a wolf. If you want to check a cello for wolf tones or *wolfs*, play the notes D3 to F♯3 on both the G- and the C-strings. Occasionally, other pitches may produce wolf tones too. Try playing close to the bridge to bring out mild wolf tones.

Spring-mounted weight
A wolf tone is the result of (a part of) the instrument vibrating at a speed that is very close to the note you play, as you will see below. A popular device used to fight wolf tones is basically a spring-mounted weight that compensates (and thus suppresses) these 'disturbing' vibrations. This device is to be installed inside the instrument.

Other solutions
In some cases, the wolf can be eliminated by attaching a short metal tube to the relevant string between the bridge and the tailpiece. The best position is determined by trial

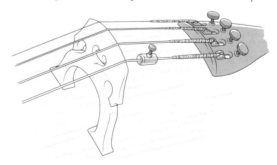

A wolf tone eliminator in action.

and error. A mild wolf can possibly be suppressed by using a mute; by changing to a heavier or lighter bridge; by mounting a fractional-sized tailpiece; by choosing lower-tension strings; or by replacing chromium-wound strings by tungsten- or silver-wound strings, for example. Putting a cork between the tailpiece and the top may work too, but this will also muffle the instrument's sound. Applying more pressure to the bow or clamping the cello with your knees as you play can prevent the wolf from becoming too active.

How it works
If you want to know more about wolf tones, here's how it works – in very basic terms. At a particular note, (parts of) the instrument may start resonating very strongly at a frequency very close to the note you play. If you play E3, for instance, the string vibrates 165 times per second. If the instrument has a very strong resonance at, say, 160 vibrations per second, the wolf will stutter five times per second (165 minus 160).

(Dis)appearing wolfs
Fighting a wolf is a matter of changing the relevant resonant frequencies of the instrument, which you do by adding weight. In some cases, the reverse may work as well. For example, violin makers have suppressed wolfs by shortening the fingerboard. As wolf tones may disappear by making changes to the instrument, certain repairs may also produce wolf tones. Replacing a bass bar is one of them.

Fine instruments
Ironically, cheap instruments are not very often plagued by wolf tones, simply because they don't have responses strong enough to cause them. Conversely, fine instruments hardly ever come without them.

9. TUNING

A cello has to be tuned before you can play it. When you start out, your teacher will help you tune your instrument, but sooner or later you'll have to learn to do it yourself. Is it difficult? No, but you'll only learn properly by doing it often. This chapter covers some basic techniques and tuning tips and tricks.

On a well-adjusted cello, steel or synthetic strings don't easily go out of tune. Even so, you always need to check the tuning before you start playing.

Steel strings and fine tuners

With steel strings, even the slightest rotation of a peg translates into a major difference in the tension on the string. That's why most steel-stringed cellos have fine tuners in the tailpiece (see page 39).

Pretune

If you use steel strings, the tuning pegs are used only to roughly 'pretune' the strings. When doing so, make sure the fine tuners are in their middle settings, so you can use them to tune both up and down.

Plucking or bowing?

You can sound the string you are tuning by plucking, as you would with a guitar. For beginners that may be easier, but you can hear what you're doing better if you bow the strings.

The A

When you hear an orchestra or an ensemble tuning, their

reference pitch is the A that you find to right of Middle C on a piano. This A is referred to as A4.

An octave lower

The A-string of a cello sounds an octave lower: It is the A *to the left* of Middle C, also known as A3. All these notes are clearly shown on the piano keyboard on page 11.

A piano at hand?

If you have a piano at hand, you can adjust the pitch of the A-string to this particular A on the piano.

Tuning fork
Tipcode CELLO-009

Usually, however, there will be no piano around. In that case, you can buy a tuning fork – a thick, two-pronged metal fork. Tap it on your knee, gently put the stem against your ear or on the bridge of your instrument, and you'll hear the reference pitch A. This pitch can be played back on many electronic metronomes and electronic tuners too.

Tuning fork in A=440.

A4

Tuning forks sound the pitch A4, while your A-string is supposed to sound the pitch A3, an octave lower. This difference makes it a little more difficult to hear whether the A-string is tuned too high (*sharp*), too low (*flat*), or just right – especially if you're just starting out.

The same pitch
Tipcode CELLO-010

Comparing your A-string to the reference pitch becomes easier if you make the string sound an octave higher. You can do this by playing the string while lightly touching it exactly midway, without pressing it against the fingerboard. If the string has been properly tuned, the *harmonic* you hear now sounds A4 exactly. Learning to play harmonics takes a little practice, but it's a very helpful technique for tuning.

Tuning the A-string

If the A on the cello sounds too low compared to your reference pitch, you'll have to raise the tension on the string by turning the fine tuner clockwise – and vice versa. If you can't hear whether the string sounds flat or sharp, try turning its fine tuner all the way down. Then you can be almost certain that it sounds flat. From there, slowly bring the pitch up.

Singing

You can also sing along. First listen closely to the reference pitch and sing it. Then sing the pitch produced by the string. Usually, you will then 'feel' if you have to sing higher or lower, and you can adjust the string accordingly.

In the middle

If you start with the fine tuners in their middle settings, you can typically tune each string up or down a whole tone or even more. In most cases, this is enough to get them to the correct pitches.

The D   Tipcode CELLO-011

Once the A is right, tune the D-string. On the piano keyboard on page 11 you can see that this D is five white keys to the left of A3. This tonal difference or *interval* is called a *perfect fifth*.

Twinkle

If you don't have a piano at hand, you'll hear this interval when you sing the first two words of *Twinkle, Twinkle, Little Star*. To tune your D-string to your A-string, you should sing the first *Twinkle* when playing the D, and the second, higher-sounding *Twinkle* when playing the A-string.

Backwards

On the cello, all adjacent strings are a perfect fifth apart. As you usually tune from high to low (starting with the A-string, then the D, etc.), it may help to learn to sing *Twinkle, Twinkle* backwards: Sing the second *Twinkle* while playing the higher-sounding string, and match the lower-sounding string to the first, lower-sounding *Twinkle*.

Check

When you have tuned all four strings, check them once more. Usually you'll have to adjust the tuning here or there. The nursery rhyme will point you in the right direction. However, there is a better way to check the tuning.

Better still   Tipcode CELLO-012

The trick is to bow two adjacent strings. On a properly tuned cello, these string pairs produce a pleasant, full sound. If they sound slightly 'wavy,' the strings are not quite in tune, so carefully adjust one of them. These 'waves' are known as *beats*. The slower these beats get, the closer in pitch the strings are. As soon as the strings are in tune with each other, the beats are gone.

Press the string

If you still can't tell if a string sounds flat or sharp, try pressing it very close to the nut. This raises its pitch very slightly. If this makes the pitch difference smaller (the beats become slower), you have to bring the string's pitch up a little. If it increases the pitch difference (the beats speed up), of course you need to slightly lower the string's pitch.

Again: harmonics   Tipcode CELLO-013

Pitch differences (and the 'waves') between two strings become even clearer if you use harmonics again. If you lightly touch the A-string exactly midway, and the D-string at one-third of its length, you'll find that they both sound a harmonic at the pitch A4. If not, you have to adjust one or both strings.

The other strings too

This trick works for the other adjacent string pairs too: Play the harmonic at one-third of the lower-sounding string, and compare it to the one midway the adjacent higher-sounding string. You can easily play these two *touch harmonics* simultaneously, using your ring finger on one string and your thumb on the other.

Too much noise

To be able to hear your strings' pitches even onstage while everybody else is tuning too, simply press one of the tuning pegs of the bass strings to your ear. Works great.

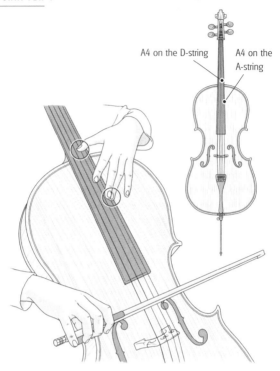

A4 on the D-string   A4 on the A-string

Comparing string pitches with harmonics.

Left or right

Some cellists operate the fine tuners with their right hand, which may be awkward as you hold your bow in that hand too. Others prefer to do it with their left hand, which requires you to move your arm around the neck first. The advantage of left-handed fine tuning is that you can bow while you tune, which makes it easier to compare pitches. A tip: You may inadvertently press the fine tuners when operating them. If so, the pitch will drop as soon as you let go of them.

Bowing

When you're tuning, try to make sure you bow with a consistent, light pressure. If you don't, the tuning may turn out to be less than perfect as soon as you start playing.

With a piano

You can of course tune all your strings to the relevant keys of a piano, but you'll learn to tune better if you use the reference A only. After all, that's how you'll often have to do it if you play in an orchestra or in another group or ensemble.

Press the pedal

If you do tune to a piano, always use the right (sustain) pedal. This will make the note sound for a long time, so the pitches of the piano and your cello are easier to compare.

Pitch pipe

Pitch pipes are popular tuning aids. There are two types, those with one note (the A) and those with four (one for each string). Pitch pipes are cheap, but their pitches usually aren't very reliable.

Chromatic tuner

An electronic *chromatic tuner* tells you exactly which pitch it is hearing, and whether it is flat or sharp. These devices, available for twenty-five dollars and up, are especially popular with guitarists. Cellists often say it's better to learn to tune by ear, because you also depend on your ear to tell you whether you are playing in tune.

Stretching strings

Strings stretch as they get older. Eventually they may come to a point where your fine tuners can't get them in tune anymore. If so, you'll have to tune them a little higher with your pegs. Before you do, first loosen the string with the fine tuner as far as it will go. Tip: If a string has been stretched this far, chances are it needs to be replaced.

Tuning with pegs   Tipcode CELLO-014

When using the pegs, it's also easiest to tune up, rather than tuning down. So if a string sounds sharp, first turn the peg until it's flat and then go back up from there, turning the peg backward in very, very small increments. Apart from that, tuning with pegs is really the same as tuning with fine tuners – though it does take some time to learn how to adjust them. One tip: Pressing the peg in while tuning will help keep it from slipping.

Seasons

Learning to tune with the pegs, even if you use steel strings, has the added benefit that it will help prevent the pegs from getting stuck when humidity is high (in the summer) or from suddenly slipping – and thus causing string damage – when the air is dry, in wintertime.

A=440 Tipcode CELLO-015

The A (A4) that most orchestras and ensembles tune to vibrates 440 times per second. This pitch is usually referred to as A=440 hertz. A well-tuned cello A-string vibrates exactly half as fast (A=220).

A=442 Tipcode CELLO-016

Some orchestras tune to an A that is a tiny bit higher. You can buy tuning forks for these tunings too, such as A=442.

Scordatura

For some works, mostly modern compositions, cellos are required to be tuned differently. Such alternative tunings are known as *scordatura*. These tunings may make playing certain chords easier, for instance. Three examples are A, D, A, D; A, D, F♯, B; and A, D, F, C (from high to low).

Detuning?

A final tip: Do not release the tension of strings after playing, as this will hurt rather than protect your instrument and the strings.

10. CELLO MAINTENANCE

Repairing and adjusting a cello are best left to an expert. But there is plenty you can do yourself to keep your instrument in the best possible condition: cleaning, replacing strings, straightening the bridge, finding buzzes, and much more.

The rosin from your bow settles on your cello as dust. You can easily wipe most of it off with a soft, lint-free cloth each time you finish playing. A cotton cloth will do fine – an old, unprinted T-shirt for instance, or a dishcloth. Be careful not to snag the edges of the instrument. On some finishes (*i.e.,* synthetic finishes) you can also use a slightly damp cloth, if necessary. Don't forget to wipe off the bow stick as well.

Fingerboard and strings
It's best to use a different cloth for the neck, strings, and fingerboard, where you touch them with your fingers. Wipe the strings with the cloth and then pull it between the fingerboard and the strings. Again, a cotton cloth is good for the job, but some cellists prefer to use silk. Once you've cleaned your cello, put it back in its case or bag.

Clean hands
Strings will live longer if you wash your hands before playing, and your cello will be easier to keep clean if you hold it only by the neck.

String instrument cleaners
Every cello needs extra attention once in a while, even if you

are very careful. The top can get sticky and dull, especially between the *f*-holes, where most of the rosin dust ends up. You can remove this residue with a special string instrument cleaner. There are string instrument cleaners and cleaning cloths that polish your cello as well, smoothing away fine scratches.

The best?

Which is the best cleaner for your cello may depend on its varnish, so always ask what you can and cannot use on an instrument when you buy or rent it. Before using a cleaner, always read the instructions. Then try a small area first, preferably one that's out of sight: Some delicate varnishes can be damaged by an abrasive polish, or by a cleaner that contains harsh solvents.

Never

Whatever you do, never use ordinary household cleaners. One exception would be using a window cleaner on a synthetic or alloy tailpiece – as long as you spray the cleaner on a clean cloth first, rather than directly on the instrument.

The fingerboard

You can occasionally give the fingerboard an extra cleaning by dabbing it with a soft cloth, moistened with a tiny bit of rubbing (or denatured) alcohol. To make absolutely sure that no liquid gets onto the varnish of the body, keep the bottle well out of the way and do not allow the cloth to drag over the body. For safety's sake, lay another, dry cloth over the body.

The strings

To remove rosin residue, grime, and finger oils from your strings, you can push a clean cloth along them a few times, going from the top of the fingerboard to the bridge. Don't push too hard, and hold one hand across the strings, because they can really screech when you do this.

Alcohol and steel wool

If this doesn't work, you may moisten the cloth with some rubbing alcohol, provided you don't use gut strings. Again, do not spill any of this liquid on the instrument. Special string cleaners are available as well. Some technicians remove rosin buildup with very fine steel wool. Always be sure to cover your instrument first before cleaning the strings!

Inside

Over the course of the years, dust and dirt will inevitably find their way inside your cello. To get it out, some cellists pour in a handful of dry, uncooked rice and gently shake it through the body a few times. The rice can be removed by turning the instrument upside down, and carefully shaking it – which makes the rice clean the underside of the top at the same time. Most of the dust will come out with the rice. A warning, though: This technique is not without the slight risk that a grain gets caught in, for example, a tiny gap between the lining and the side and causes a rattle, especially in roughly made or frequently repaired instruments.

Splinters

When cleaning the instrument, make it a habit to check for splinters, especially around the edges, and other minor damage. The cleaning cloth or your clothes can pull these splinters off of the instrument, or the splinters can hurt you, or your clothes may get caught in them while playing…

Expert

You need to take your cello to an expert when it needs more extensive cleaning, if there are stains that won't go away, if you can't get the neck clean, or if the varnish has become very dull (on the body, under the strings, or where you touch the body with your left hand). Many cellists have their instruments checked once a year, even if nothing seems to be wrong, just to be on the safe side.

Plastic

If your perspiration is especially acidic, it can damage the varnish and even the wood of the ribs where your left hand touches it. The solution? There are violin makers who stick a strip of self-adhesive plastic to the rib. Others makers are appalled at the very idea of sticking plastic to an instrument. As an alternative, you can try using a cloth or velvet bib.

TUNING PEGS AND FINE TUNERS

Fine tuners do not require much maintenance, if any at all. If one does get a little stiff, you may apply a tiny bit of acid-free Vaseline. Wooden tuning pegs, on the other hand, can be troublesome.

Peg compound

The tuning pegs need to be able to turn smoothly, without slipping back. This usually requires the periodic use of a little *peg compound* or *peg dope*. Other cellists prefer tailor's chalk, also known as French or Venetian chalk. If these treatments aren't effective anymore, you can clean the peg and peg hole with a little benzene. A stopgap solution for slipping pegs is to apply white chalk – but this will make the hole wear out faster. Some types of soap are being used too, but soap may congeal and make tuning harder.

Loose

If a peg or the hole is badly worn, the peg can get really loose. Having a new set of bigger pegs custom-fit to the instrument will usually cost some hundred and fifty to two hundred dollars. This may or may not include the pegs, available from around seventy-five to a hundred dollars for a set. There are much more expensive pegs too, with golden rings or other decorations. If the peg holes are really worn out, they can be (re)bushed.

BOW

Maintaining your bow basically comes down to applying rosin to it, and very occasionally you should have the bow hair thoroughly cleaned. Rehairing is, of course, a job for a professional.

Rosin   Tipcode CELLO-017

Applying rosin is necessary only when the bow hair gets too smooth. That won't be more often than once or twice every week, even if you play a lot. Move the bow hair over the rosin rather than the other way around, applying the rosin along the full length of the hair, from the head to the frog. Keep your thumb on the ferrule to prevent it from damaging the rosin, and cradle the rosin so that you can extend several fingers above it to guide the bow.

Rosin walls and fingers

Three more tips: Prevent the bow hair from wearing a groove in the rosin (which will eventually leave 'walls' of unusable rosin) by rotating it now and again. The second tip is not to touch the bow hair or the rosin with your fingers, as finger oil and perspiration keep the rosin from holding onto the bow hair. If you need to touch the bow hair, *e.g.*, to check the tension, do so with the back of your hand. Tip number three: When using a brand new cake of rosin, some like to scratch its surface with a pin to 'get the rosin started.'

Excess rosin

After applying the rosin, wipe the bow hair with a cloth, or drag one of your nails across the bow hairs close to the frog. This ensures that the excess rosin doesn't land on your instrument. You can shake out your bow instead, but it's best not to: Even if you don't break anything or hit anybody, whipping the bow around in the air can damage it. A tip: If your sound becomes coarse or uneven after applying rosin, you used too much of it.

Grimy near the frog

If the bow hair gets grimy near the frog, you can clean it with a lukewarm, damp cloth, possibly with a little liquid soap in the water. If you do, be careful that the little wooden wedges that hold the hair in place are kept dry. If they get wet, they may expand and damage the stick.

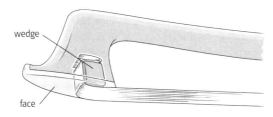

The bow hair is held in place by small wooden wedges.

Cleaning the hair

If you need to apply rosin more and more often, that's probably due to old bow hair (have it replaced) or to a buildup of rosin residue, which makes the hair slick. Some cellists clean the hair themselves, using a cloth that's very lightly moistened with rubbing alcohol – but it is much safer to have it done by an expert. The liquid can easily damage the stick, and you may end up with the bow hair sticking together, rendering the bow unplayable. A bow maker or technician can decide whether cleaning will help, or if rehairing is necessary.

New hair
If the bow hair is overstretched, you'll never get the bow back to proper tension. The usual solution is a rehair. The same is true if too many of the hairs have broken. A rehair often costs some forty or fifty dollars. Sometimes, the bow hair can be shortened. Good-quality hair will last for years, and won't become wavy or brittle.

Not tight
If you can't get the hair to the desired tension, the bow hair may be overstretched, or your bow stick could be slowly loosing its curve. A bow maker or technician may be able to restore the curve.

Broken bow hair
If a hair breaks, remove the loose ends by cutting them against the sharp edge of the ferrule or the face, rather than pulling them out. Another solution is to cut them carefully with scissors, as close as possible to the ferrule or face.

Smooth frog
If the frog doesn't slide smoothly anymore, and the screw button feels stiff, cleaning them may help. Just turn the screw button counter-clockwise until it comes off. Then you can remove the frog too. If the problem persists, it's best to have the bow looked at, which you should also do if the bow grip needs to be replaced, or if the frog wobbles. Two final tips: Be very careful not to get your bow hair twisted if you remove the screw and frog. Never use oil to lubricate the screw or the *underslide* (the part that lines the top of the frog), but gently rub them with a candle.

REPLACING STRINGS
If strings break or if their windings come loose, you need to replace them. The same is true if they're getting old: Old

strings get more and more difficult to tune, and sound duller and duller. The better your cello is, the better your playing and the better your ear, the sooner you'll notice when strings need to be replaced.

One string only?

If you replace a single string, you may find that it sounds a lot brighter than the older ones. If so, the only solution is to replace the other strings too. A tip: Used strings may still be useful as spares.

Not more than two

If you want to replace your strings, never take off more than two of them at a time, so that the tension of the other two keep the bridge and sound post in place. If the sound post still falls over, loosen all the strings and have it set in position by an expert, who has a special tool for that purpose.

The right order

The two outer strings pass below the middle ones in the pegbox, which makes them harder to get to. So first loosen one of the middle strings, and then the string that passes below it. Now replace the outer string, and then the middle one. An example: Take off the D, then the G; first replace the G, then the D; and proceed similarly with the other two strings.

Removing strings
Tipcode Cello-018

To replace strings, sit down and lay the cello with its scroll on your left or right thigh, whichever is easiest for you. Take off the first string by slowly turning its tuning peg

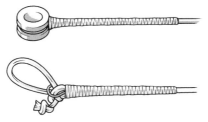

Most strings are attached to the tailpiece with a steel ball; gut strings often have a loop instead.

forward to release the string's tension. If the peg doesn't move, pull it out slightly. Then pull gently on the string, so the peg will start turning until the string comes loose. Guide the string between your thumb and index finger near the pegbox, so that it can't suddenly come loose and cause any damage.

Fitting strings
Tipcode Cello-019

You can fit new strings in various ways. This is one simple way.

1. Turn the first peg so that the hole points diagonally upwards, facing the fingerboard.
2. Hook the ball end of the string in the fine tuner, or in the tailpiece slot. If the string has a loop end (gut strings) hook the loop in the tailpiece slot. Do not feed the string through its loop as if it were a lasso – unless the slot is worn out so it doesn't hold the string.

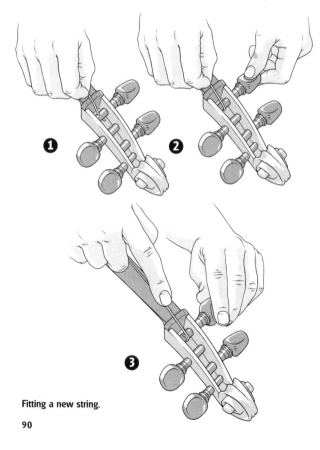

Fitting a new string.

3. Stick the string through the peg hole (see illustration 1) and start winding it, turning the peg backward so the peg hole moves in the direction of the scroll.
4. Hold the string with your other hand so that it can't go slack and slip out of the peg, or come loose from the tailpiece (illustration 2).
5. Keep tightening the string, making sure that the windings run outwards, toward the thicker end of the peg. Use your index finger to keep the string tight and guide it through the groove in the nut (illustration 3). Also, make sure that the string doesn't wedge up against the inside of the pegbox.
6. Tune it so that it is at roughly the right tension, using the strings that are still in place for reference.

Kink

If a string keeps on slipping off the peg hole as you try to tighten it, take a pair of pliers and make a kink about half an inch (1–1.5 cm) from the very end of the string. The kink will make the string hook itself in place as you begin to turn the peg.

Firmly fixed

There's another way to be sure your strings will stay firmly fixed. Make a kink in the same way as before, stick the

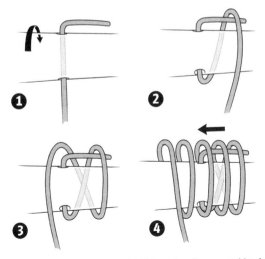

Make a kink in each string. Lay the kink against the peg, and let the unwound part of the string wind around it a couple of times.

string through the peg's hole, and then lay the kinked end flat against the peg. Guide the string so that it runs over the kinked end a couple of times as you turn the peg. A warning: Do not wind the plain (non-wound) part of a wound string around itself.

Too long

If a string happens to be very long, you can first make sure it winds inwards for a few turns before guiding it back the other way. The last few turns must be wound directly onto the wood, and not on top of another part of the string. Tip: Four or five windings should be enough to prevent a string from slipping.

Space

Strings can break if they are jammed against the cheeks of the pegbox. So always make sure they have some space.

String sleeves

If you use string sleeves (see pages 55–56), slide them into place when the strings are nearly tuned.

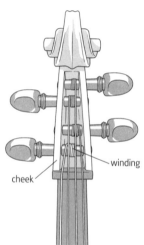

cheek

winding

The first time

When you replace a string for the first time, you'll probably be short of hands. You need one to tighten the string;

Leave space between windings and cheeks.

another to make sure it doesn't come loose from the tailpiece; a third to guide it through the grooves in the bridge and nut... So have someone else around to help.

Grooves

When you replace your strings, check the pegs at the same time. Grooves in the pegs can damage your strings. If a peg won't 'grip' the string whatever you do, there's a chance that its hole is worn out.

Sharp edges

Your strings can also be easily damaged by sharp edges on

the bridge, the nut, or around the string holes in the pegs. The grooves in the nut must be smooth and nicely rounded to prevent the strings from kinking. Check your cello carefully if a string keeps breaking at the same point. If a string doesn't run smoothly across the nut or the bridge, twist the point of a soft lead pencil through the groove a few times. If that doesn't do the trick, you'll need expert help.

Different strings

If you want to fit other types of strings than the ones you have used so far, there are some things to pay special attention to. First, if the new strings are thicker (for instance, if you replace steel strings with synthetic strings), the grooves in the nut and the bridge should be wide enough not to catch the strings and damage the windings. Second, fitting higher-tension strings will raise the string height, and vice versa. This can be compensated for by adjusting or replacing the bridge, for instance.

Perfect fifths

If you have a good ear, there's another way to find out it your strings need to be replaced. On a properly tuned cello, there is always a perfect fifth between one string and the next (see page 78). You can check this by using a pencil to stop two adjacent strings in exactly the same position: Lay the pencil at a right angle across the two strings, and press them against the fingerboard. In both high and low positions, the difference in pitch between the two strings should always be a perfect fifth.

Old strings

If you have old strings, this may not be so, perhaps because one string is more stretched than the other. If so, the first will sound flat. Old strings are not the only possible cause if you don't hear perfect fifths; the bridge may be the culprit instead. Another tip: If you use gut strings, you may not hear perfect fifths with this test either.

THE BRIDGE

A cello bridge has to withstand a lot of force, the strings' tension both pulling it forward and pushing it into the body – so you do need to keep an eye on it.

Perpendicular

Now and then, you should check that the bridge hasn't started leaning forward, toward the fingerboard. If it does, you can carefully try to push it back in its original position yourself, until its back is perpendicular to the instrument's top. Before doing so, first release the string tension a bit. A tip: Don't hesitate to leave this to a violin maker or technician.

Perfect fifths

Another check: Make sure that both feet are lined up with the notches in the f-holes. If not, your instrument will not produce perfect fifths (see the previous page) and it will be hard to play in tune.

New bridge

A bridge needs to be replaced if the downward pressure of the strings has forced it to bend, or if the grooves have got too deep: No more than a third of the diameter of each string may be inside the groove. A new type of strings may require another bridge too. Another reason to have your bridge changed or replaced is that its top is too flat (so that you accidentally play two strings instead of one), or too curved (making it difficult to play two or three strings at once). A tip: Some violin makers may restore a bent bridge, which is cheaper than having it replaced.

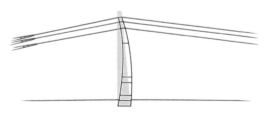

Bridge bending toward the fingerboard.

Summer and winter bridges

Dry winter air can make the wood of your cello shrink, in which case string height will be reduced. By the same token, higher humidity in the summer can expand the wood and increase the height of your strings. To compensate for these changes, you can use two bridges: a higher one for the winter, and a slightly lower summer bridge.

Custom-fit

A new bridge needs to be custom-fit to the cello, so that it has the right height and curve for the instrument, and so that its feet match the top perfectly. Having a new bridge installed by a professional violin maker will often cost between seventy-five to hundred fifty dollars, the bridge itself costing less than the labor involved in installing it. A new bridge should last for years.

More than carving alone

There are bridges with moveable feet that automatically adjust to the arch of the top. Even if you prefer this type of bridge, you should have a specialist install it: Again, properly fitting a bridge to an instrument involves more than carving the feet.

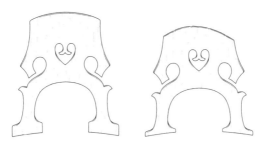

A blank bridge (left) and one made to fit the instrument.

AND THE REST...

A cello is a fragile instrument that only gives its best if everything is in place, nothing that might produce a buzz is loose, and nothing is worn out.

The sound post

If you have bought a new cello, it's a good idea to have it checked after six months or a year. One example of what an expert might spot is that the sound post may have become slightly too short as a result of the wood not having settled completely when you bought the instrument.

The tailpiece loop

Another example would be that the tailpiece loop may have stretched. If so, the distance between tailpiece and bridge will now be too short, which may muffle the sound.

On a full-size cello, the correct distance is about 4.5–5" (11.5–12.5 cm, *i.e.*, ⅙ of the instrument's string length). To set this distance, tailpiece loops are often adjustable.

The fingerboard

However hard your fingerboard is, stopping the strings will eventually make grooves in it. Even your fingers will eventually make shallow pits in it, especially if you perspire a lot. Of course, if you have a good, ebony fingerboard, this is a very slow process. Professional cellists, who play for many hours every day, often have their fingerboards reworked once a year or every two years. Replacing a fingerboard is expensive, because a lot of labor is involved.

Loose pieces

If a piece of your cello breaks off, for instance along the edge, make sure that no moisture reaches that spot, and don't clean it. Take the instrument to a violin maker as soon as possible, and take the broken-off piece with you if you still have it. It's also best to see an expert if you find loose glue joints, or cracks. Tempted to glue them yourself? Don't!

Buzzes

A cello can start buzzing in all sorts of places. Some examples:
- If the bridge or the nut is **too low**, the strings may vibrate against the fingerboard.

Purfling can work loose and cause buzzing.

- The **winding** of a string may be damaged.
- The **string ends** may vibrate if they are touching the pegbox or tailpiece.
- While checking the tailpiece, have a look at the **fine tuners** too – especially the lock nuts.
- A **wire mute** or loose **purfling** can also cause unwanted noises, and so can an eye, or a decorative button on a tuning peg, or a loose **glue joint**.

HUMIDITY

Wooden instruments are very sensitive to dry air, and to rapid changes in humidity or temperature.

Freezing

Dry air is especially likely to be a problem if it is freezing outside and the central heating is on full blast. If humidity gets too low, the wood of your instrument will shrink. The result? If you're lucky, you'll only find that the string height is reduced, and that you need a winter bridge (see page 94). If you're less lucky, the tuning pegs may suddenly come loose, which can result in string breakage, and it may get even worse: The top, the back, or any other parts can crack. The faster the humidity changes, the more dangerous it is.

Hygrometers

The best level of humidity, both for cellos and for people, is often said to be around fifty to sixty percent. A hygrometer is a device that allows you to keep an eye on the humidity level. You may have one in the room where you keep your cello, and some cello cases have one built-in. If the hygrometer shows that the air is getting too dry or too moist, it's time to do something about it.

Humidifiers

First, there are all kinds of small humidifiers that can be used inside the case, ranging from a very basic rubber tube with holes in it and a small sponge inside, to more complicated devices. Dampit is the best-known trade name. Prices are between about five and fifteen dollars, which sometimes includes a very basic humidity indicator. Cases with a built-in hygrometer often feature a humidifier as well.

Sluggish

A dial-type hygrometer, which uses a hair to measure the humidity level, may become sluggish and less responsive after about a year. To solve this, leave it outside for a night, and the moist air will refresh it for a whole year. When the weather gets colder and you switch the heating back on, you can also wrap it in a wet cloth for a quarter of an hour and immediately afterwards set its pointer to 98%.

All-around solutions

If humidity is very low in your house, then your instrument, your wooden furniture and floors, and yourself may benefit from a central humidifier (if your heating system allows for one) or a portable one. Some examples of the latter are steam humidifiers (affordable, work fast, but may be noisy) and 'cold' humidifier systems, which are quieter but more expensive, take longer to work, and may need frequent maintenance (cleaning, filling, and so on). If humidity is very high, you may get a dehumidifier instead.

Some time to adjust

Always give your instrument some time to adjust to changes in temperature and humidity. For example, if it's freezing cold outside and you enter a warm room, leave your instrument in its case for fifteen minutes, or as long as you can. The more gradually things change, the better your instrument will like it. Another tip: Always put your cello back in its case or bag as soon as you stop playing.

Heaters and vents

Some don'ts: Never store a cello in direct sunlight, or near heaters, fireplaces, air-conditioning vents, or anywhere else where it may get too hot, too cold, too dry, or too wet – not even if it's in its case.

ON THE ROAD

A few tips for when you travel with your cello – which includes visiting you teacher:

- Make sure you have **a good case or bag**, and check now and again to make sure that the handles and carrying straps are properly secured.
- In the car, your cello is usually safest **on the back seat**.

- **Never leave your instrument in a car** for any length of time. Heat can rapidly build up and cause damage.
- Flying out? See if you can carry your instrument **as hand luggage**.
- If you do leave your cello behind somewhere, you're more likely to get it back if your **name**, **address**, and **phone number** are listed inside the case or bag.
- Just to be on the safe side: Always have a set of **spare strings** with you.

Insurance

Consider insuring your instrument, especially if you're taking it on the road. Musical instruments fall under the 'valuables' insurance category. A regular homeowner insurance policy will not cover all possible damage, whether it occurs at home, on the road, in the studio, or onstage. Companies that offer special insurances for musical instruments can be found in string players' magazines or on the Internet (see pages 125–127). They may require that you have your instrument appraised before insuring it. Two final tips: Most insurances do not cover climatic damage; always check the policy on the conditions for air travel.

11. BACK IN TIME

Nobody really knows when the first cello was made, and there are many, often contradictory stories about its history. In this chapter, you'll find only some of the better known highlights of the instrument's origins. The details can be found in many other books.

In the days when dinner was still something you hunted, humans discovered that shooting an arrow produces a tone, due to the vibration of the bow's string.

The eighth century

Only much later was it discovered that you can also make a string vibrate by bowing. Bowed instruments were probably being played in ancient Persia as early as the eighth century, and were brought from Arabia to Spain not that much later. One of these instruments, referred to as either *rebab* or *rebec*, is often considered the ancestor of the violin family.

Viols and violins

Eventually, two groups of instruments emerged from the rebab: the *violas da gamba* or *viols*, and the members of the violin family.

Arms and legs

The violin family is closely related to the earlier *lira da braccio*. In fact, braccio instruments were played exactly like the violin – 'on the arm', as the Italian word *braccio* indicates. The violas da gamba, on the other hand, were played with the neck in an upright position; their bodies

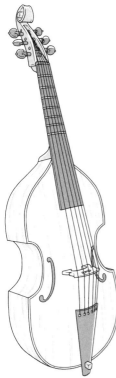

Viola da gamba, a bowed instrument with frets and six strings.

rested on or in between the legs of the musician – *gamba* is Italian for leg.

Not the gamba

As you hold the cello between your legs too, people often think it stems from the viola da gamba. It doesn't, however: Violas da gamba are quite different. They have sloping shoulders and a flat back; they have C-shaped soundholes and more strings, which are tuned differently. They also have frets, like a guitar. These small ridges on the fingerboard make playing in tune easier.

Violone

The cello was based on the violin, really. When Flemish composers started to use lower-sounding voices in their works, some time in the fifteenth century, musicians needed lower-sounding instruments than the violins and violas of that time. Consequently, various larger versions of the violin were built. These instruments were initially known as *bass violins* or *violones*, the latter being Italian for 'large violin.'

Small large violin

The instrument that eventually became the cello was not the largest of these instruments – so the Italians called it *violoncello*, which literally means 'small large violin…' Only much later, around 1765, was the term violoncello abbreviated to cello or 'cello. When talking about the very first cellos, people often refer to the instrument shown on a fresco from 1535 by the Italian painter Ferrari.

Andrea Amati

Andrea Amati is usually considered the first maker of cellos, and some of his instruments are still around.

Amati's cellos were of a quite large design, with a body of about 31.5" (80 cm). These larger instruments are often referred to as *church basses*.

Antonius Stradivarius

The development of the slightly smaller, modern cello started in the late seventeenth century. Musicians wanted a smaller instrument because it would be easier to play: The string tension would be lowered and the distance between the positions on the fingerboard reduced.

Around 1707, Stradivarius, still the world's most famous violin maker, started to make these smaller cellos. Eventually, he created the standard model that's still being used by makers today.

Violins versus viols

It took the cello a long time to replace the viola da gamba. For many years, the members of the violin family were looked down upon by the upper class. They were used for dance music, at parties, and in parades, while 'serious' music was played on the more delicate and softer-sounding violas da gamba. Incidentally, the viola da gamba is still being used today to play the music of that era.

Solo

For many years, the cellist's role was solely to accompany other instruments – one of the reasons why it has been called bass or bass violin for so long. Antonio Vivaldi (1678–1741) was one of the first composers to write cello solo concertos. The first compositions for unaccompanied cello date back to the late seventeenth century. The violin was used as a solo instrument long before the cello.

End pin

The end pin was probably introduced in the 1840s by the Belgian cellist Adrian Servais. Until then, the instrument usually rested on the player's calves.

The bow

The very first bows had an outward curve, like the type of bow you shoot arrows with. Slowly the design changed to an inward curved stick. Around 1790, François Tourte (see page 64) designed the standard for today's bow.

From gut to synthetic

Wound strings were already in use in the mid-seventeenth century. Steel strings became popular in the 1920s, followed by synthetic-core strings in the 1950s.

12. THE FAMILY

The violin and the viola are the cello's closest relatives, followed by the double bass. Most other bowed instruments are either traditional or ethnic instruments, from the rabab to the kemenche and the Hardanger fele. The youngest relative, the electric cello, is covered at the end of this chapter.

Tipcode Cello-020

As was explained in the previous chapter, the cello is a descendant of the violin. It's not just a bigger violin, though. If you would apply the violin's dimensions to the cello, its body would have to be about about 40" long (much longer than it is), and it would only be some 3.5" deep. Such instruments, usually referred to as *tenor violins*, have been built but they were never successful.

The viola

The viola is just a bit larger than the violin. It's tone is slightly lower, and also a bit darker and fuller. A viola is tuned to the same notes as a cello, but an octave higher: The A-string sounds the same pitch as the reference pitch most musicians tune to (A4).

The double bass   Tipcode Cello-021

The double bass, the lowest-sounding bowed instrument, looks like a mixture of the violin family and the viola da gamba. For example, it has the *f*-shaped toneholes and the fretless fingerboard of the violin and the cello, but its (usually) sloping shoulders stem from the viol family. A bass is tuned differently as well, the strings being a fourth apart, rather than a fifth. They're tuned to E, A, D, G, from

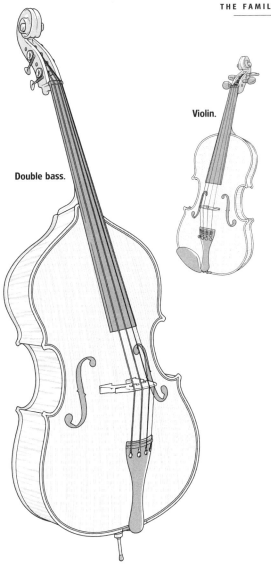

Violin.

Double bass.

low to high, just like a bass guitar. The double bass is often used outside classical music, in which case it is usually plucked instead of bowed – again, like a bass guitar.

ETHNIC AND TRADITIONAL INSTRUMENTS
Most of the other members of the bowed string family are quite rare, and you'll usually find them only in the hands of ethnic musicians or musicians who play older styles of music.

Bourdon strings

The *viola d'amore*, for instance, is one of the bowed instruments that has a set of regular strings as well as some *bourdon strings*. These strings are not bowed or plucked, but they vibrate sympathetically with everything you play. The lira da braccio (see page 100) had bourdon strings or *off-board drones* as well.

Fele and rabab

There are many other bowed instruments with bourdon strings. The Norwegian *Hardanger fele* is a smaller type of violin that has four of them, and there are no less than twelve bourdon strings on the Afghan *rabab* shown below.

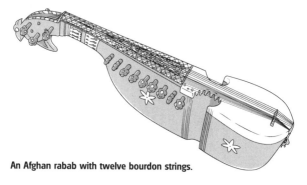

An Afghan rabab with twelve bourdon strings.

Many names, many shapes

As discussed in the previous chapter, the predecessor of the violin was also called rebab. Today, this name is used for a wide variety of bowed instruments, some with and some without bourdon strings.

Kemenche, kamaché, kemângeh

The same goes for the *kemenche*. This name may refer to a small, pear-shaped instrument with three strings used in Turkish classical music. But it can also indicate an elongated three-stringed instrument used to play folk music around the Black Sea and in Greece. The spelling varies as much as the shape, from *kemânje* to *kamaché* and *kemângeh*, and similar instruments are sometimes referred to as rebabs (or *rababs*, *râbabs*, and other spellings) as well. They're mostly played with their tail on the knee of the musician, with the neck held upright, like a viola da gamba. Incidentally, you may even see musicians who play a regular violin that way. And today's *rebecs*? They come with two, three, or more strings, with various body shapes, with or without frets...

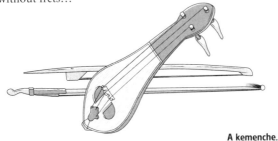

A kemenche.

With a fingernail
On some of these instruments, the different pitches are made not by stopping the strings on the fingerboard, but by touching them very lightly with a fingernail. The bow stick is often straight, and you tension the bow hair not with a frog but simply by putting your fingers or thumb between the stick and the hair.

Many more
Many other cultures have their own bowed instruments too, from one-stringed Indian to tubular Native American models. The format of this book doesn't allow listing them all, but there are other books that do.

CELLO VARIATIONS
Many variations on the cello have been designed over the ages. Most of them disappeared within a decade or so after they were introduced; others lasted a little longer, but none survived as long as the current members of the family.

Piccolo and tenor
In between the cello and the viola, for example, was the four- or five-stringed *violoncello piccolo*. *Violoncello tenor* is one of the names used for instruments that sound an octave lower than the violin – just as the cello sounds an octave lower than the viola.

Portable cellos
Other cello variations were developed to improve the instrument's portability. One design, the *violoncello*

portatile, had a detachable neck that could be stored inside the rectangular body of the instrument. The *porta cello*, built around the middle of the twentieth century, featured a smaller, though traditionally curved body and retractable knee rests.

Indian music

Making variations on the cello is not a thing of the past. Today's models are usually one-of-a-kind, custom-built instruments. One of the numerous examples is a five-string cello (D, A, D, A, D) with ten bourdon strings, designed to play Indian music.

ELECTRIC CELLOS

If you play your cello in a band, you're likely to find that it isn't loud enough. This can be solved by using a regular microphone, but you can also add pickups to your instrument, or even buy a cello that's designed to be played amplified only.

Electric/acoustic

You can amplify your instrument by supplying it with one or two *pickups* or *transducers*. These small, flat 'sensors' are usually wedged between the wings of your bridge. They literally pick up the vibrations of the strings and convert them to electric signals that can be amplified. As this solution allows you to play your instrument unamplified (acoustically) too, you could consider it an *electric/acoustic* cello.

Clip-on microphone

Some types of transducers (i.e., *piezo pickups*) can make your instrument sound less warm and natural than a microphone would. That's why some cellists prefer to use a miniature clip-on microphone. However, using a microphone can easily cause feedback (the loud *skreee* you also hear if you point a microphone at a loudspeaker), especially if you need to play really loud. A best-of-both-worlds solution is to use a pickup as well as a (vocal) microphone on a stand; there are also systems that combine a pickup and a clip-on microphone, with a control to set the balance between the two.

Electric cellos

If you plan to play electric only, you can consider buying an electric cello. These instruments have no soundbox, but a small, often solid body instead. Played without an amp, you hardly hear a thing. This makes them ideal for silent practicing sessions. Some electric cellos were specifically designed for that purpose (see page 17).

Chest and knee rests

To be able to hold the small-bodied instrument just like a regular cello, most electric models come with chest and knee rests. Usually they're detachable for easier transportation and storage.

MIDI

Some electric cellos can be hooked up to synthesizers, effects devices, computers, and other digital equipment, using a system called MIDI (*Musical Instrument Digital Interface*).

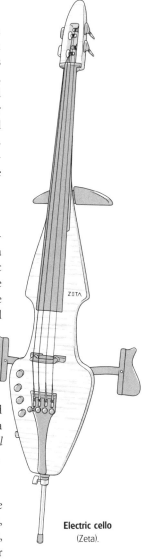

Electric cello
(Zeta).

Shapes, designs, and prices

Electric cellos come in a wide variety of shapes and designs, often with more than four strings, and with tuning machines rather than the traditional wooden pegs. Some brand names in this field are Jensen Instruments, New Epoch, NS Design, Starfish Designs, Strauss, T.F. Barret, Violectra, and Zeta. Prices range from a thousand to seven thousand dollars and up.

13. HOW THEY'RE MADE

Good cellos are still made in much the same way as they were hundreds of years ago, with chisels and files, with saws and planes, and with glue. Making a cello top in the traditional way easily takes a master violin maker several days' work.

Tipcode CELLO-022

In a string instrument factory, machines are used for parts of the process, such as roughly shaping all the wooden

components. Master violin makers who build an instrument by themselves from start to finish, still do everything by hand. Somewhere in between these two extremes are the workshops that buy unvarnished *cellos in the white*, which are finished by hand and provided with fittings and strings.

Quarter-sawn wood is stronger that slab-cut wood.

Cake

The top and back are usually made of *quarter-sawn* or *quartered wood* – wood that has been sawed from the tree trunk in the shape of slices of cake. Each slice is then sawed almost in half to enhance the drying and seasoning process of the wood, which will make it less likely to warp, split, or shrink later on.

Bookmatched

This slice is later sawed through completely to make two

halves. These are folded open, like a book, and then glued with their backs together. The result is the beginning of a *bookmatched plate*, the two halves being each other's mirror images. Not all plates are bookmatched.

Carved

Traditionally, the top and the back are then carved into shape. Using dyes and thickness gauges (graduation calipers), and simply by feel, the violin maker keeps checking to see if any more wood needs to be removed.

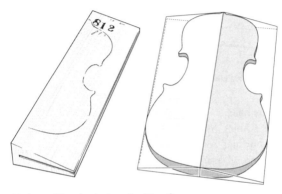

Folded open like a book, then glued together.

Ribs, blocks, and lining

The ribs of the instrument are either moistened or heated so they can be shaped, then glued to the top, bottom, and

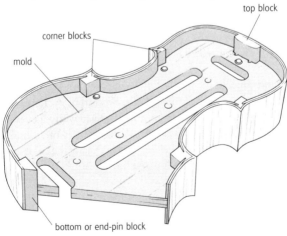

... assembled around a mold...

corner blocks that strengthen them at the joints. The rib structure is assembled around a wooden mold. Small strips of woods (the lining) where plates and ribs meet are necessary to properly glue these parts together.

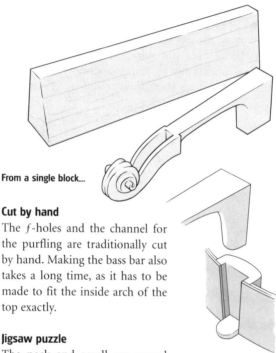

From a single block...

Cut by hand

The *f*-holes and the channel for the purfling are traditionally cut by hand. Making the bass bar also takes a long time, as it has to be made to fit the inside arch of the top exactly.

Jigsaw puzzle

The neck and scroll are carved from a single block of wood. The

Jigsaw puzzle...

neck slots into the top block like a piece in a jigsaw puzzle. The weight of the fingerboard, which is made of heavy ebony, is reduced by hollowing out the underside.

Mirror-smooth

Before it can be varnished, the wood has to be made mirror-smooth with a scraper. It is finished with a base coat and several coats of varnish. Violin makers often make their own varnish, so they can give it exactly the color and characteristics they are looking for.

Bows

The bow stick is cut by hand, and its camber is shaped over a flame. The horsehair is held in place in the frog and head by small wooden wedges.

Wonderful stories

There are lots of wonderful stories told about secret methods used by makers of those expensive old Italian cellos. For instance, it is said that the wood used to make them was transported by dragging it behind a sailing ship, and that it is the salt seawater that gives the instruments their special sound. Others say that the wood comes from centuries-old church towers that burned down; the wood was first broken in by vibrations from the church bells and then ripened by the fire… Or perhaps the varnish is the greatest 'secret' of those old cellos – and the secret is safe, because the materials that were used back then are no longer available today.

14. BRANDS AND MAKERS

When you go out to buy a cello, you'll come across dozens of brand names – names of violin makers young, old, or dead, names of violin makers who never even lived, brand names and names of countries, towns, and regions. This chapter sheds some light on the cello market, and it introduces you to some of the famous old masters.

Germany has long had a great reputation for producing good instruments in every price range. As a result, many cellos bear a German name, even though they have been made in other European countries or 'overseas,' the latter usually referring to various Asian countries, from Korea to Sri Lanka. Italian names are popular too, based on the rich cello heritage of that country.

Brand names

Also, a certain brand name may be given to cellos made by various different workshops or factories – or a single brand name may be used for cellos with components from three different countries, which are assembled in a fourth country, varnished in a fifth, and shop-adjusted by the distributor or dealer. So brand names on cellos do not often tell much about the instrument's origins.

Quality

On the other hand, of course, there are many companies whose (brand) names can be seen as a guarantee for a certain quality. Some examples would be **Becker**, **Otto Brückner**, **F. Cervini**, **Glaesel**, **Knilling**, **Meisel**, **Pegasus**, **Scherl & Roth**, and **Wm. Lewis & Son**, and other names mentioned in this chapter. Please note that these lists are not intended to be complete, and that brand names can be discontinued, sold, or changed.

Germany
The German towns of Bubenreuth, Mittenwald, Klingenthal, and Markneukirchen are famous for their violin-making traditions and for the instruments made there today. A few of the better-known names are **Götz**, **Höfner**, **Paesold**, and **Stein**.

Eastern Europe
Many of the founders of German string instrument companies came from the Czech city of Luby, which is often referred to as the 'Czech Mittenwald.' Other Eastern European countries, such as Hungary, Romania, and Bulgaria also have long cello-making traditions, from master instruments to low-priced, factory-made student cellos. Some brand names include **Dvorak**, **Lidl**, and **Strunal** (Czech Republic), **Grygo Petrof** (Bulgaria), and **Bucharest** and **Vasile Gliga** (Romania). The Romanian center of violin making is Reghin.

Asia
Cellos from China, Korea and other Asian countries have long had a poor reputation, but their quality is improving all the time. Chinese cellos especially are rapidly getting much better, with many of the better ones being built of German wood. Some examples of Chinese companies would include **Ren Wei Shi**, **Samuel Shen**, and **Xue Chang Sun**. Still, most of the Asian instruments can be found in the lower price ranges. **Nagoya Suzuki** is one of the better-known Japanese brands, mainly known for their fractional instruments.

France
France no longer produces large numbers of cellos, but two hundred years ago the French town of Mirecourt was home to the world's first string instrument factory, employing some six hundred people. The prices of old French factory-made instruments are usually a little higher than those of comparable German cellos. The French ones sound a little louder and brighter than the German

models, some say – and others claim to hear the opposite.

Other countries

In most countries you'll be able to find master violin makers who create high-quality instruments entirely by hand, usually to order. Most of them also sell used instruments, bows, and accessories, and they repair and rebuild instruments too.

(Master) violin makers

Not everybody who uses the name 'violin maker' is a master violin maker. Some mainly do repairs of student and intermediate cellos, or they specialize in expensive instruments only; others concentrate on finishing and setting up white cellos (see page 110), and so on. The exact number of master violin makers is unknown, but there must be over a hundred of them in the US alone. Most countries have an association or federation of violin and bow makers, which you'll be able to trace on the Internet or in string players' magazines (see pages 125–127).

OLD MASTERS

Many books list the stories of dozens or hundreds of violin makers from the past, where and when they lived and worked, and what their instruments could be worth today. Even then, there's a good chance that the maker of your old cello won't be mentioned, simply because there are too many of them. Here's a very short introduction to some of the most famous names.

Italy

The most famous Italian cellos were built in the town of Cremona, from the sixteenth century onwards. **Andrea Amati**, who presumably died in 1577, was one of the first violin makers. His grandson **Nicolo Amati** taught the craft to **Francesco Ruggieri** (also spelled as Ruggeri; 1620– c. 1695), the most famous member of another important Cremonese violin-making family. Another of Nicolo's pupils was **Antonio Stradivari** (often referred to as Stradivarius), who lived from 1644 to 1737. Stradivarius also made harps and guitars. Of his bowed instruments, around six hundred have survived. **Domenico Montagnana**

(c. 1680–1750) and **Joseph Guarnerius del Gesu** (1698–1744), the best-known member of the Guarnerius family, were among Stradivarius' students.

Outside Cremona

Apart from the Cremonese school, to which all of these violin makers belonged, there were also other schools. Each had its own characteristics, such as the shape of the *f*-holes, or the precise model of the body or the scroll. The double purfling was one of the characteristics of the Brescian school. This school was founded by Gasparo di Bertolotti, known more commonly as **Gasparo da Salò**.

Germany

Jacob Stainer, who died in 1683, is often seen as the founder of German violin making. Until well into the eighteenth century, an instrument made by Stainer was more expensive than a Stradivarius; the latter was often considered 'too loud.' **Mathias Klotz I** (1656–1743), who was very important for violin making in Mittenwald, studied under Stainer and Nicolo Amati. Instruments made by his sons Sebastian and Georg are still highly prized.

Other countries

Two important French makers were **Nicolas Lupot** (1758–1824) and, from Mirecourt, **Jean Baptiste Vuillaume** (1798–1875). One of the best-known English names is **Hill**, a company where various violin makers and bow makers worked. You often find the description 'Hill model' on tailpieces, tuning pegs, mutes, and other parts. **Hendrik Jacobs** (1630–1704) and **Johannes Cuypers** (1766–1828) were two of the main Dutch makers. Some of the early American makers were **August Gemünder**, **Abraham Prescott**, and **Benjamin Crehore**.

GLOSSARY AND INDEX

This glossary contains short definitions of all the cello-related words used in this book. There are also some words you won't find on the previous pages, but which you might well come across in magazines, catalogs, and on the Internet. The numbers refer to the pages where the terms are used in this book.

Adjuster See: *Fine tuners* and *Screw button.*

Antiquing *(27–28)* Technique to make cellos look older than they are.

Back, back plate See: *Flamed wood* and *Top.*

Baroque cello *(34, 51)* Special, mellow-sounding gut-stringed cello to play the music of the Baroque era.

Bass bar *(9)* Wooden bar on the inside of the top.

Belly See: *Top.*

Body *(5, 6, 29–31)* The body consists of the top, the back, and the sides.

Bottom nut See: *Saddle.*

Bow *(9–10, 57–64, 86–88)* Cellos are played with a bow. The bow is very important for the sound of the instrument. See also: *Bow hair, Frog,* and *Stick.*

Bow grip *(10, 60)* Piece of (synthetic) leather around the stick of the bow, used also to indicate the (silver, silk, or imitation baleen) *winding* or *lapping* next to it. Also known as *thumb grip.*

Bow hair *(9, 58, 87–88)* The hair of the bow; either horsehair or synthetic. Also known as *ribbon.*

Bridge *(6, 7, 34–37, 93–95)*

The strings run over the bridge, which passes their vibrations on to the top.

Button See: *Heel.*

C-bout *(6, 29)* The waist of the body.

Catgut The oldest material used for cello strings – sheep gut. The name comes from *cattle gut.*

Cello in the white *(110, 116)* Unfinished cello.

Channel *(6, 8, 31)* The 'valley' near the edge of both the top and the back before the upward arching begins.

Cheeks *(6, 48)* The sides of the pegbox.

Children's cellos *(12–13, 56)* See: *Fractional sizes.*

Curl See: *Flamed wood.*

Double bass *(2, 104–105)* The lowest-sounding string instrument.

Ebony See: *Wood.*

Electric cello *(17, 108–109)*

An electric cello can be plugged straight into an amplifier, just like an electric guitar.

End pin *(6, 7–8, 41–43)* The cello rests on a retractable, adjustable rod mounted in a (usually) wooden plug (*end button*). Plug and rod are collectively referred to as the end pin. Also known as *spike.*

End screw See: *Screw button.*

Eye, Parisian eye *(38, 59)* Inlaid decoration on tuning pegs, frogs, and other parts. A Parisian eye is a mother-of-pearl dot with a small metal ring around it.

ƒ-hole *(5, 6, 117)* The soundholes of a cello are shaped like an *ƒ.*

F-stop See: *String length.*

Figured wood See: *Flamed wood.*

Fine tuners *(6, 7, 38, 39–40, 76)* Small, additional tuning mechanisms in the tailpiece. Also referred to as

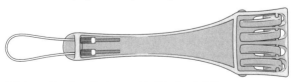

Tailpiece with adjustable loop and built-in fine tuners.

tuning adjusters, string tuners, and *string adjusters*.

Fingerboard *(5, 6, 31–33, 96)* When you play, you press down or *stop* the strings against the fingerboard.

Fittings Collective name for the cello's replaceable parts, *e.g.*, tailpiece, pegs, and nut, but the fingerboard as well. Also known as the *trim*.

Flamed wood *(28)* Many cellos have a back and ribs which look as though they have been 'licked by flames.' This *flamed, figured*, or *curled wood* is usually more expensive than *plain wood*.

Fractional sizes *(12–13)* Cellos in small or *proportional* sizes, designed for children. Fractional-sized instruments require fractional-sized strings *(56)*.

Frog *(10, 58, 59)* One end of the bow hair is held in place inside the frog. The *underslide* lines up with the top of the frog. At the bottom of the frog is the *slide*. Most frogs are *full-lined* with a metal *back plate*. At the front, where the hair enters the frog, it passes through the *ferrule* or *D-ring*.

Full-size cello *(12)* The regular, 4/4-size cello. See also: *Fractional sizes*.

Fully-carved *(111)* Fully-carved instruments have tops and backs made by carving only.

Hair See: *Bow hair*.

Heel *(8)* Semi-circular projection of the back, strengthening the joint of the body and the neck. Also referred to as button.

Insurance *(99)* A good idea.

Lining *(111–112)* Thin strips of wood glued to the inside edges of the body.

Luthier Another name for a (master) violin maker.

Maple See: *Wood*.

Master cello *(21–22)* Built by a master violin maker from start to finish.

Mensur ratio See: *String length*.

Mountings *(58)* The metal parts of a bow.

Mute *(16, 71–74)* A mute makes your sound a little sweeter and softer. *Practice mutes* muffle the sound a lot.

Neck *(6, 32–34)* The long wooden section that extends from the body. The fingerboard is attached to the neck.

Nickel silver *(58)* Mixture of copper, zinc, and nickel. Also known as *alpaca*.

Nut *(6, 7, 32)* The wooden strip over which the strings run at the top end of the neck. Also called *top nut.*

Parisian eye See: *Eye, Parisian eye.*

Peg, Pegbox *(5, 6)* The (tuning) pegs are fit into the pegbox. See also: *Tuning peg.*

Peg compound, peg dope *(86)* Lubricant for tuning pegs.

Pegging The process of fitting the tuning pegs to the instrument.

Pickup *(108)* Small, thin sensor that converts the vibrations of your strings into electrical signals, so that you can plug your cello into an amplifier.

Plain wood See: *Flamed wood.*

Plates The back and the top or table of the instrument.

Practice mute See: *Mute.*

Proportional instruments See: *Fractional sizes.*

Purfling *(6, 8, 28–29)* Inlaid decoration, which also protects the top and back.

Quartered wood, quarter-sawn wood *(110)* If you saw a tree trunk or sections of it into quarters (the way you would cut a cake into slices), you get stronger wood than if you *slab-cut* the tree. Because quarter-sawn wood is stronger, it is good for making thin yet strong tops and backs.

Ribbon See: *Bow hair.*

Ribs *(29)* The sides of the body.

Romberg *(32)* Romberg fingerboards have a flat area under the C-string.

Rosin *(10, 64–67, 86–88)* Without rosin to make the bow hair sticky, your bow will do nothing at all.

Saddle *(6, 7)* A strip, usually of ebony, that prevents the top from being damaged by the loop that holds the tailpiece in place. Also known as *bottom nut.*

Screw button *(10, 58, 59)*

Used to tighten and relax the bow hair. Also called *end screw* or *adjuster*.

Scroll *(5, 6, 28)* The decoration at the top of the neck. Also known as the *maker's signature*.

Slide See: *Frog.*

Sound post *(9, 37–38)* Thin, round piece of wood wedged between top and back. Referred to as the 'soul' of the cello.

Spike See: *End pin.*

Spruce See: *Wood.*

Stick *(10, 57–58)* The wooden – or synthetic – part of your bow.

Stop See: *String length.*

Stradivarius *(23, 102, 116)* Antonio Stradivari, often referred to as Stradivarius, is the world's most famous violin maker. He also built the standard model for the cello.

String adjusters See: *Fine tuners.*

String height *(34, 54, 94, 97)* The distance from the strings to the fingerboard, measured at the end nearest the bridge.

String length *(12, 29)* Usually refers to the length of the strings between nut and bridge, also known as their *speaking length*. Violin makers also use the term *f-stop*, referring to the distance from the top edge of the body to the notches of the f-holes. The ratio between the distance from the body's edge to the notches and from the nut to the edge is referred to as the *stop, neck to stop ratio*, or *mensur ratio*. In cellos that ratio is usually 10:7, but differences may occur, even between cellos with identical string lengths. A tip: A deviant mensur ratio can make you play out of tune.

String tuners See: *Fine tuners.*

Strings *(10–12, 49–56)*, **replacing strings** *(88–93)* Cello strings are available in gut, synthetic-core, and steel-core versions, and with windings made of all kinds of metals.

Table See: *Top.*

Tailgut See: *Tailpiece, tailpiece loop.*

Tailpiece, tailpiece loop *(6, 7, 41)* The strings are attached to the tailpiece, and the tailpiece is attached to the end button with the tail-piece loop or *tailgut (95–96)*.

Top *(5, 6, 29–31)* One of the most important components of a cello: the top of the body, also known as *table* or *belly*. The opposite side is the *back*.

Top nut See: *Nut*.

Trim See: *Fittings*.

Tuning *(38–40, 76–82)* Cellos are tuned using the tuning pegs or the fine tuners.

Tuning adjusters See: *Fine tuners*.

Tuning pegs *(5, 6, 38–40, 86)* Cellos are tuned using four (tuning) pegs, often in combination with one or more fine tuners. The peg head is known as the *thumb piece*. See also: *Fine tuners*.

Underslide See: *Frog*.

Varnish *(27)* The varnish used is important for the sound and the appearance of your cello, and for the way you need to clean it.

Viola, violin *(2, 104, 105)* Two very close, much smaller relatives of the cello.

Volute See: *Scroll*.

White cello *(110, 116)* Unfinished cello.

Winding See: *Bow grip* and *Wound strings*.

Wolf tone *(74–75)* This stuttering effect, by which many cellos are plagued, can be suppressed in many different ways.

Wood *(28, 30, 31)* The main types of wood used for cellos are spruce (for tops), maple (for backs and sides) and ebony (for fingerboards, tuning pegs, tailpieces, and other parts).

TIPCODE LIST

The Tipcodes in this book offer easy access to short movies, photo series, soundtracks, and other additional information at www.tipbook.com. For your convenience, the Tipcodes in this Tipbook are listed below.

WANT TO KNOW MORE?

Tipbooks supply you with basic information on the instrument of your choice, and everything that has to do with it. Of course, there's a lot more to be found on all subjects you came across on the previous pages. A selection of magazines, books and websites, as well as some information on the makers of the Tipbook series.

MAGAZINES

The following two magazines offer lots articles on cellos, violin makers, strings, playing, and much more.

- *Strings*, phone (415) 485-6946,
  www.stringsmagazine.com.
- *The Journal of the Violin Society of America*, phone (845) 452-7557, www.vsa.to (also see below).
- *The Strad* (UK), phone +44 (0)141 302 7744,
  www.thestrad.com.
- *American Lutherie*, fax (253) 472-7853, www.luth.org (stringed instrument making and repair; covers guitars and other fretted instruments as well).

BOOKS

There are dozens of books on the cello. The following is a brief selection of publications that cover some of the subjects of this Tipbook in greater depth.

- *Cello (Yehudi Menuhin Music Guides)*, by William Pleeth (Kahn & Averill, 2001; 290 pages; ISBN 1 871 08238 2).
- *Cambridge Companion to the Cello*, Robin Stowell (editor) (Cambridge University Press, 2000; 269 pages; ISBN 0 521 62928 4).

- *Cello Story*, by Dimitri Markevitch (Summy Brichards Inc., 1984; 182 pages; ISBN 0 874 87406 8).
- *The Cello*, by Elizabeth Cowling (B.T. Batsford, 1975; 224 pages; ISBN 0 713 42879 1).
- *The Health of the Violin, Viola & Cello: Practical Advice on the Acquisition, Maintenance, Adjustment, & Conservation of Bowed Instruments*, by Lucien Greilsamer (Henry Strobel, Violin Maker and Publisher, 1991; ISBN 0 962 06734 2).

Making a cello
There are quite a few books for amateur and professional violin makers, which also can be of interest if you just want to know more about the instrument. Some examples:
- *Cello making, step by step*, by Henry Strobel (1995; ISBN 0 962 06737 7). This book should be used with *Violin making, step by step* (1994; ISBN 0 962 06736 9). The author and publisher of these titles, Henry Strobel, wrote various other books on the subject as well.
- *Violin Making: A Guide for the Amateur*, by Bruce Ossman (Fox Chapel Publications, 1998; 96 pages; ISBN 1 565 23091 4).
- *Violin and Cello Building & Repairing*, by Robert Alton (Library Binding; 182 pages; ISBN 0781205174).

INTERNET
On the Internet, you'll find countless sites for cellists, often with all kinds of links, articles, discussion groups, and FAQs. Following are some good starting points:
- Internet Cello Society (www.cello.org).
- New Directions Cello Association (www.newdirection-scello.com).
- American String Teachers Association (www.astaweb.com).
- Violink (www.violink.com).
- Maestronet (www.maestronet.com).
- American Federation of Violin and Bow Makers (www.afvbm.com).

Smithsonian Institution
Of course, you can also check out whether there is anything on the maker of your cello by searching the Internet on that

name. If you are interested in the great old masters, take a look at The Smithsonian Institution's site at www.si.edu/resource/faq/nmah/music.htm.

ORGANIZATIONS

The Violin Society Of America (VSA; 1974) promotes the art and science of making, repairing, and preserving the instruments and bows of the violin family. The VSA organizes an annual convention that features speakers, demonstrations of instrument and bow making and repair, performances, and more. For information call (845) 452-7557 or visit www.vsa.to. The VSA also publishes a journal (see above) and a quarterly newsletter.

Violin makers

If you want to locate a professional violin maker, you can contact the American Federation of Violin and Bow Makers (www.afvbm.com).

THE MAKERS

Journalist, writer, and musician **Hugo Pinksterboer**, author of The Tipbook Series has published hundreds of interviews, articles and instrument, video, CD, and book reviews for Dutch and international music magazines. He is the author of the reference work for cymbals (*The Cymbal Book*, Hal Leonard) and has written and developed a wide variety of manuals and courses, both for musicians and for non-musicians.

Illustrator, designer, and musician **Gijs Bierenbroodspot** has worked as an art director for a wide variety of magazines and he has developed numerous ad campaigns. While searching in vain for information about saxophone mouthpieces, he got the idea for this series of books on music and musical instruments. He is responsible for the design and the illustrations of all of the books.

ESSENTIAL DATA

In the event of your instrument being stolen or lost, or if you just decide to sell it, it's useful to have all the relevant data at hand, either for yourself, your insurance company, or for the police. You can jot down this information on these two pages. There's also room to list the strings you're currently using, for future reference.

INSURANCE

Company:

Phone: Fax:

Agent:

Phone: Fax:

Policy number:

Insured amount:

Premium:

CELLO

You'll find some of the details of your cello on the label, which – if there is one – is usually visible through the f-hole on the side of the C-string. Some cellos have labels that can only be read when the body is opened. The name of the maker can also be branded in the body, for example on the back, close to the heel.

Make and model:

Manufacturer/violin maker:

Serial number:

Color:

Make of bridge:

Tailpiece   make:

                   type:

                   color/material:

Description of tuning pegs:

Any repairs, damage, or other distinguishing features:

Date of purchase: Price:

Place of purchase:

Phone: Fax:

BOW

Make/maker:

Type: Price:

Octagonal/round:

Mounting:

Date of purchase:

Place of purchase:

Phone: Fax:

STRINGS

It's worth making a note of the strings you put on your cello, so you can use the same ones again if you like them – or avoid them if you don't.

string	make	type	thickness/tension	date
1st: A				
2nd: D				
3rd: G				
4th: C				

string	make	type	thickness/tension	date
1st: A				
2nd: D				
3rd: G				
4th: C				

string	make	type	thickness/tension	date
1st: A				
2nd: D				
3rd: G				
4th: C				

ADDITIONAL NOTES

....

....

....

....

....

....

....

....

....

....

....

....

....

....

....

....

TIPBOOK SERIES
MUSIC AND MUSICAL INSTRUMENTS*

Released

Tipbook Acoustic Guitar
Tipbook Cello
Tipbook Clarinet
Tipbook Drums
Tipbook Electric Guitar and Bass Guitar
Tipbook Flute & Piccolo
Tipbook Piano
Tipbook Saxophone
Tipbook Trumpet & Trombone
Tipbook Violin & Viola

Expected in 2002

Tipbook Music on Paper – Basic Theory
Tipbook Vocals

Want to know what's available today?
Take a look at www.tipbook.com.